# Diversions and Delights in

# Costa del Sol

Two Old Fogies Divert Disasters and Experience Culinary Delights in Southern Spain…

And Share Delicious Andalusian Recipes!

## LELE BEUTEL

Two old fogies are up to their adventurous antics again as they travel through southern Spain. Captivated by the sensational scenery, they encounter historical places and tasty delights. From fantastic food and remarkable restaurants to people-friendly pueblos, you'll sigh and salivate along with them. So, tag along for this memorable, and sometimes surprising, adventure through Costa del Sol.

Dedicated to those who enjoy seeing new scenery and experiencing delightful dishes, especially my siblings, all foodies, who, despite the challenges, will travel the distance to savor a great meal.

Our first night in Spain at El Pimpi Restaurant

# ALSO BY LELE BEUTEL...

***Lessons from The Cotswolds,*** *Two Old Fogies Dodge Disasters while Walking Through the Cotswolds*

***The Camino Connection,*** *Connecting with Life and Commemorating a Death while Walking on the Camino de Santiago*

***What God Wants You to Know,*** *A Daily Devotional*

***God Answers,*** *A Daily Devotional*

***Lele's Selah,*** *Prayerful Poems that Inspire Hope*

***The Reignbreaker,*** *A young adult fantasy*

***Flora's Story,*** *A young girl and her family survive the Nazi and Russian regimes of 1940s Germany*

# TABLE OF CONTENTS

# INTRODUCTION

I *started to sweat in my seat on the bus....*
The tour guide had just reminded everyone that they needed a passport to experience the amazingly famous Rock of Gibraltar. And I had forgotten to bring ours!

"Everyone has theirs? Right?" the guide asked, smiling in his own blasé way.

"Oh no!" I muttered under my breath, after digging furiously through my bag. I started to hyperventilate. "I didn't bring ours! *What do we do?*"

The bus had already left the resort, and we were well on our way to "The Rock."

"I can't say anything now!" I whispered to myself. "I definitely DO NOT want to make the bus driver turn around and go back! Not when we're this far along! *Arg!!!* How awful is this? And *embarrassing!*"

As I gazed out the window, I thought of all the possible options. Frantically, I looked through my phone, thinking I had a copy of the identifying passport pages. I remembered being told to take a picture of these in case we lost them. But they were nowhere to be found. Apparently, I hadn't saved them. I looked through the notes on my phone, searching for passport numbers. They were there. But would these count? Along with a driver's license? Maybe the officials would make an exception.

The severe sweating continued as I turned to let Mike, my husband, know the gory truth.

"I forgot to bring our passports!" I tried to speak loud enough for him to hear over the roar of the bus, but not so full-throated that others could detect my anxiety…or stupidity.

Unfortunately, since we'd left so early for this day-long trip, everyone was deathly quiet, reclining sleepily. My words, if spoken too loud, could be heard by everyone around us. I heard munching from the seat in front of me, and I detected the cheddary smell of cheese and the crunching sound of crackers, so I knew at least one person was awake. I tried to keep my voice as low as possible. But sadly, I was sitting on the side of my husband that held the ear without the cochlear implant. He could barely make out my words.

"*Wha-a-a-t!*" his voice raised. "*I can't hear you!*"

"I forgot the passports!"

After I uttered the words, my own voice escalated, I could feel my face turning bright red when the munching sound from the seat in front of me suddenly stopped. Then my heart started palpitating so fast it felt like it might burst through my chest. *Had others heard me too?*

"I still can't understand you!" Mike blurted out, irritated that I'd chosen to sit on his non-hearing side.

But my hearing had shut down as my eardrums kept time with my thumping heart, like an out-of-control set of bongo drums. My mind raced, and I wondered if anyone else could hear the rhythmic beating that reverberated from inside me. *Dang!*

*Well,* I thought, trying to calm myself down, *the worst thing that can happen is we get kicked off the tour!*

And that is precisely what happened!

This longed-for trip was part of a very generous retirement package from my company. Out of all the choices for places to go, my husband and I decided on Costa del Sol, a sun-drenched area of a region called

Andalusia in Spain. We'd experienced other areas of the country. In 2017, we cruised through scenic ports along the northern coast, from Santiago de Compostela to San Sebastian, and I'd walked across northern Spain in 2023. But we'd never ventured into the southernmost parts, and we were looking forward to seeing as much as we could.

Andalusia is Spain's southernmost autonomous community known for its rich history, diverse landscapes, and vibrant culture. Known for its beaches, warmth, and gorgeous golf courses, Costa del Sol, in Andalusia, is literally "Coast of the Sun," a world-renowned tourist destination. I knew, based on past company-sponsored trips, that we'd stay in an "over-the-top" venue—a place so expensive that we could never afford it on our own. I'd discovered, over the years, after qualifying for a number of these excursions, to expect top-notch service. This included local people driving us from the airport to our destination and accommodations in four- or five-star-rated hotels with rooms so extravagant that it almost took your breath away. The food was always wonderful to the point that we hated to come home to our usual fare!

One downside to these lovely, arranged tours was that we often stayed in places so exclusive that the only contact we had with the local people was through connections with the staff! To me, this was unfortunate, especially after experiencing the Camino de Santiago, a pilgrimage through northern Spain, which I wrote about in *The Camino Connection*, where I encountered many locals and people from all over the world. I hoped that, somehow, we'd still meet some from the area to get the real, true flavor of the place. Would God work that out for us?

Another concern caused me even greater consternation. Since it was my last company-sponsored journey, I wondered if I'd recognize anyone. I used to know many in the company and see some of the same people on every tour. But so many of my closest friends had retired. *Would there be anyone on this trip I knew?* I wondered.

Granted, the wild card on every voyage was always the travel and what might happen that we did *not* expect. We'd learned by experience that, no matter how thoroughly you planned, you had to be ready for the unexpected—the things you could never anticipate, no matter how much you planned. *Would we make our connections? Would we have the seating we wanted? How far did we have to walk to get to the next flight, and would we make it in time? Would we have what we needed, and who would help us if we needed help?* At our ages—eighty-two and seventy-two—these were important questions, and more pertinent now than ten or twenty years ago.

But I'd also realized over the years that somehow we would always manage to survive even the most unexpected events, with God's help. Knowing this, we prayed before the trip, because we knew He'd have to help us along the way. This excursion was no exception, as you will see!

## Chapter One
# THE TRIALS AND TRIUMPHS OF TRAVEL

Barney looked up at me with sad, pleading eyes as an attendant took his leash from me at the kennel. My heart lurched as I turned away, trying to ignore our shweenie (half shi tzu, half dachshund). I glimpsed his beseeching stare then turned my head away quickly as I waved goodbye to the ladies at the counter. As much to him as to them, I yelled, "I'll be back!" sounding a little like Arnold Schwarzenegger in *The Terminator*.

We'd landed a nice day for travel. I tried to focus on that blessing instead of the guilty feeling in the pit of my stomach I wanted to quash as we drove away from the kennel. Traveling internationally, we needed to be at the airport three hours before our flight. We got to the ticket counter with plenty of time to spare. Proud of our promptness, I was greeted by a somewhat flighty desk agent. Her eyes averted, she seemed confused and didn't bother to print off our boarding passes. I asked her about the necessary tickets. Her response?

"Get them at the gate!" she said tersely.

That didn't seem right.

*Hmmm,* I muttered. *Never had to do that before!*

When I asked a lady at the gate for our flight to please print them for us, she was obviously annoyed.

"Didn't they print them off at the ticket counter?" she huffed.

"No, ma'am," I tried to be polite.

"Well, you'll just have to wait 'til closer to the time of takeoff," she smacked.

It was 9:00 am and our flight would depart at 11:10 am. I waited patiently. When I returned to the gate counter to get our passes at 10:40, there was a very long line! Several irked people in front of me fussed, gripping their passports. Apparently, they'd encountered the same woman at the first ticket counter.

*Wonderful!* I mumbled.

Besides this unexpected hassle, I faced another issue. That morning, before we left for the airport, my stomach decided to lurch and careen. I made sure I was within sprinting distance of a bathroom. Being denied an initial boarding pass and now waiting in this line of grumbling passengers didn't help my predicament. I avoided coffee, realizing the acidity made me feel worse. But steering clear of caffeine produced other not-so-great side effects. I didn't have a debilitating headache, which I usually get when I don't drink coffee. Thank God for that. But I did feel groggy. I drank water, and that helped my symptoms, but I still felt sick to my stomach.

Another alarming challenge was that, when I woke up and looked in the mirror, I was shocked to see one eye almost completely swollen shut! "Ok, God," I blurted out, *"what the heck is this?"* As I inspected my eye, I wondered how bad it was, and if it might get worse. *Should I cancel the trip and go to a doctor?* I rasped to myself. *Arg, no!* At that moment, I made an executive decision and muttered my favorite saying, "It is what it is!" Then I doused my eye with drops and salve. Hopefully, my glasses would hide the blaring, puffy atrocity!

Now, I stood in this ridiculous and avoidable line, my eyelid poofing out even more and my stomach churning, waiting to get a silly piece of paper to allow me on this flight. It was the only thing substantial enough to stand in my way to starting this latest adventure. And I was darned if I'd let this or any of these crazy airport people stand in my way!

Then I thought of what I'd tell the other older women in my prayer group, who wanted to travel but were sometimes stymied by worse issues than mine—age-related health problems. Painful joints, aching muscles, and disturbing diagnoses would flare up right before their planned excursions, causing them great concern.

"If God wants you to go on this trip," I'd say, "He'll provide a way to do it!" It was what I told my husband too, when he brought up things that might hinder our plans. I recalled the time, before leaving for my trek on the Camino, when I experienced excruciating pain in my hips and sciatic nerve. I went to a prayer night at my church the week before starting out, and I said, "God, if you want me to sit for hours on a plane and walk for miles on this journey, then You must rid me of this pain! Thanks, Lord!" Well, He did! So I felt free to offer Him yet another challenge.

"You've helped me before," I said. "I know You can do it again."

Well, I finally hit the head of the line, in time for our flight, and retrieved our passes. The flight from Kansas City to Minneapolis left the gate, and, for the first leg of our journey, my stomach felt better. I sighed with relief. Now, I'd see how He'd help me with the disturbing eye situation.

In the Minneapolis airport, we found a great Japanese/Korean restaurant called *Shoyu.* As they set bowls of broth in front of us, I breathed in the spicy, stomach-friendly fragrance of kimchi, which is known to improve gut health. I happily sucked down the soft, chewy udon noodles. They also offered us ginger and grapefruit drinks, and I was thrilled, since ginger improves digestion and relieves nausea, and grapefruit promotes healthy digestion and boosts the immune system. As I sipped the drinks and slurped the broth, I could hear my stomach shouting, *Hurray! Just what I needed!*

Delicious kimchi stew!

But now, the bad news…. We were supposed to have a "mere" two-hour layover in Minneapolis before our flight to Paris. Well, it ended up dragging on for two more hours, since the jet bridge for embarking and disembarking our plane was broken. After four hours, they finally moved us to another gate. With at least two hundred other passengers, we were packed into many rows near the new gate. I detected the smell of potato chips and sandwiches and looked around to see people chowing down hungrily in their seats. Mike and I sighed, read, got up to walk and stretch our legs, sat, and sighed again. Then we watched as airline attendants unloaded travelers one by one from our waiting plane. I wondered how the deboarding people felt about being imprisoned on the plane for two hours longer than they'd anticipated. And this after a long flight to get here. *Whew!* It made me a bit more thankful to be sitting here, free to walk around. We were told that our connecting flights in Paris, if missed, would be rescheduled. *Hmmm.* I wondered if an airline that couldn't problem-solve a broken bridge very efficiently (or print boarding passes at check-in) would be dexterous enough to fix the flights of hundreds of sidelined passengers.

During one announcement, a couple sitting across from our seats caught my eye. In their sixties, the husband was much taller than the wife, who had spiky, short, gray-streaked hair. I especially noticed how, even as an older couple, they held hands. I found this endearing. Mike and I hardly ever hold hands and, if we do, it's rarely in public. It never lasts more than a few minutes…or seconds. Was it because we were such independent or nonfeeling people? Were we too prudish or self-conscious? Just not the affectionate type? *Maybe it wasn't our "thing." Hmmm.* I pondered.

Gary Chapman, in his book *The Five Love Languages,* described the ways people express and experience emotional affection in relationships. He explained that everyone has one or more "languages." The list included words of affirmation, quality time, acts of service, receiving gifts, and physical touch. I knew Mike's love languages: touch and time. Mine were acts of service, words of affirmation, and gifts. And I thought about how neither of us, after thirty years of marriage, have really mastered these ways of expressing love to each other! Especially the touch! *Was it too late*? I asked myself. *Well, you're never too old to change,* I posited.

I recalled how my dad never hugged me, and my mom's embraces were few and far between. Was it considered unacceptable when they grew up in the 1920s, 30s and 40s? My dad's parents never cuddled or touched either. Their background was German and Scottish. *Maybe it just wasn't encouraged*, I thought. But I imagined my mom's mom *was* a hugger. Short, plump, and squishy, she lived on a farm with Pappy in South Carolina. I wish I had gotten to know her, but we never saw much of them when I was growing up. Nanny and Pappy were poor and unsophisticated, and I think this embarrassed my mom.

I embraced my kids when they were little, but, as they grew older, not so much. I think this was a big mistake on my part. Sometimes, when I see a young boy, my heart sinks. I remember the whirlwind days around my son's early years, when I was a single mom with little time to spend with him. I was too busy working to support us. Since he died at age thirty-four from lung cancer, I wish I had more days with him, especially in his younger years, when work stole so many moments away from us. I would hold his hand as much as I could and tell him over and over again how much I loved him. Now, I'd give anything to be able to hug him just one more time. A favorite memory is of him embracing me during his last days on earth. Even while he struggled to breathe, he put his arm around me as we sat together on a swing in his backyard. I realize now that he wanted to reassure me of his love and leave me with this undeniable impression. And I am so very grateful for it.

Recently, while visiting my daughter, I reached over and held her hand while we sat together, watching a movie, and I could feel both our hearts melting. She put her head on my shoulder, and tears streamed down her cheeks. I thought about how distance had separated us, how long it had been since I hugged her, and how much we both needed that kind of warm reassurance that no one else could give. I was completely captured by that moment, and I will never forget it.

I laughed now to think about how Mike, way beyond hugs and handholding, loudly protested if he discovered we were wearing the same color! "I never want anyone to think that you dress me!" he's said so many times. I always wondered about this intense reaction. Why did he find this so objectionable? Then, on a trip to Switzerland, a couple in our travel group wore matching outfits every day, with identical shirts and pants. Out of curiosity, I asked the husband why they chose to do this, and he replied, smiling, "She wants to make sure that, if one of us gets lost, she can point to her outfit and say, 'He's dressed the same as me.'"

This sort of made sense. But I couldn't think of any time this would come in handy for us. I loved matching things, like jewelry and scarves that went with my outfit, but this seemed extreme. Mike found it abhorrent. I guess we both valued our independence. Here, at the airport, I thought this couple's handholding was sweet, but very unusual. I just don't often see too many older couples (or young couples for that matter) showing this kind of affection. Including us. But I hoped that might change.

We finally boarded our plane but didn't take off until 5:30, more than two hours later than expected, and I knew we'd miss our flight out of Paris to Málaga, Spain.

"We'll see when we get there if they've rescheduled our flight," I muttered with a sneer. "God, would You work this out for good?"

We sat in the bulkhead with plenty of space in front of us, and I thought about how, as we'd aged, we realized that it just doesn't pay to fly coach. The legroom is so cramped, especially for Mike, who is six-feet-tall with longer legs. After butting our knees against the seats in front of us and being severely cramped for at least eight hours on overseas flights, we'd spend the rest of our trips trying to rehabilitate our sore legs, backs, necks, etc. So, we always opted for a step up in seating, called "comfort plus" or "premium economy." It offered more legroom and seats that often leaned back farther with a place to prop up your feet. That came in handy if you have short legs like mine.

I'd prefer to go first class when I travel. I've experienced this a couple of times, and I loved it! I sat comfortably in my own "pod" with plenty of space to store my stuff, my own closed-screen TV, and, best of all, a seat that converted into a bed with a comforter and plush pillow to boot. It was heaven! On top of these luxuries, I was handed an impressive menu for dinner and breakfast that included several wonderful options, including unlimited drinks and champagne. I was also offered a hot, refreshing towel before every meal that felt amazing to press against my face and feel the heat steaming away every care. It felt like I was being given a fancy spa treatment before I ate. And a fabulous meal was served before anyone else on the plane! It was almost unbelievable, I must say! I think everyone should experience this...at least once in their lifetime!

The downside was...drumroll...the price tag! I'd found that upgrading to first or business class came with a hefty hike in price. Instead of costing you maybe $750 for coach, you were out at least $3,500! It was hard for me to justify an extra $5,500 for a seven or eight-hour flight for the two of us! So, we compromised and paid an extra $1,900 for both of us to fly comfort plus with the extra legroom. For many on a limited budget, this would be a more reasonable option.

On this flight, we had more space, but our bulkhead seats had some hidden "features." We had to stow our backpacks in the overhead, since we couldn't place them under the seat in front of us. That meant pulling out everything we needed for the flight and stuffing it into an already packed pocket in front of us on the wall. The small TVs, attached to bulky metal arms, were difficult to pull out from beside the seats, and the screens were so lopsided that we had to watch movies with our heads cocked! Plus, the seats didn't recline any farther than in coach, and they didn't have footrests. So, I opted to read and prop my feet up with pillows on the floor during the flight. At least I was able to finish a good book!

A flimsy curtain separated us from first class. Trying to get comfortable, I peeked through a crack in the fabric as stewards brought hot, steaming towels with tongs to each privileged passenger. Then, they ushered in trays filled with fancy drinks and delectable appetizers as the first-classers beamed and luxuriated. My mouth watered and my stomach growled as they brought out pristine dishes of savory, sauce-covered meat with mashed potatoes, and green salads covered by a wine and vinegar dressing, topped with crusty croutons. My eyes squinted, trying to see every detail around the curtain, especially when I detected the fragrance of creamy chocolate cake, lemon tarts, and buttery custards. I sighed, growing impatient for my own food to arrive.

Finally, a cart rolled through the curtain and our steward thrust foil-covered containers of food onto our pulled-out tables. I tried to figure out how to unwrap mine as he blurted out, "Anything to drink?" From the limited choices, I decided on my usual—tonic water with lime. Trying to decipher what was under the foil, I finally determined it was braised chunks of chicken with rice and overcooked vegetables coated with an unidentifiable sauce. A covered cup of thick, hardened pudding sat on the side with plastic-wrapped, biscuit-like, unrecognizable cookies. *Woohoo! Yum!*

It wasn't as bad as hospital food I've had or what you might find in a nursing home, but it was a far cry from the sights and smells coming from first class.

Choices, choices, choices. Maybe next time I'd bite the bullet and pay for another upgrade! It might be worth the chance to survive another flight!

I tried to catch some ZZZs. But, every time I barely dozed off, my neck would cry out in pain from being stuck in a lopsided position, or my legs, balanced on a pile of blankets, would protest from being cramped. Sleep alluded me and never lasted more than a few minutes before some part of my body screamed, *"Ouch, ouch, ouch!"* and I had to change positions again. During the exhaustive moments I was awake, I obsessed about what would transpire when we got to Paris, and we missed our next flight because of the delay out of Minneapolis. I didn't want to worry, but I kept thinking about it. Every time I started to fixate on the problem, I reminded myself to give it to God! But then my mind started to whirl and race again. *Yippee!* Not much sleep here!

We arrived in Paris at 9:00 the next morning. It was exactly seven hours ahead of our home-time—2:00 am. After a tedious trek through winding, poster-plastered hallways to the main terminal, we were thankfully processed quickly through security. This was very different from the last time I'd travelled through Paris in 2023. Then, it was *way* more chaotic, with long wait times at gates and people packed together in circuitous lines through customs and checkpoints. Now, it seemed like they'd beefed up the process to make it more efficient. For this, I was grateful.

We followed the French and English signs toward our gate through concourse after concourse and a maze of luring shops. I caught whiffs of perfume in hundreds of shapes and sizes displayed on shelves that cascaded toward the aisles. Nicely dressed, attractive salespeople, also of different shapes and sizes, stood among the exhibits, eager for customers to make a purchase. Stores bombarded my eyes and ears with sights and sounds from a multiplicity of exhibits. Some amassed every kind of liqueur imaginable, with omnipresent signs to draw speeding travelers from the walkway toward bottles of varying shades of clear, caramel, cream, or brown liquid. Covered with fancy, metallic labels, they shouted out their special qualities and tastes—all to captivate an airport audience.

My favorite shops in foreign airports are the ones with hundreds of varieties of tempting fromage! Yes, I *do* love cheese, almost any kind, and samples are always a delight! I am like Wallace in the Claymation series, *Wallace and Gromit*, about an Englishman who adores his Wensleydale cheese and often expresses his affection with a wide-mouthed utterance, *"Cheeeeese!"* Even little bits on a plate are inviting to me. I can smell some now, especially the pungent varieties, like sharp cheddar, Limburger, Camembert, Munster, Roquefort, Stilton, or Gorgonzola… the list goes on! *Ahhh!* Sadly, we were in a hurry and had to forego any savory tastings.

When I looked, it seemed we'd have to wait until 4:25 pm for our flight to Málaga. At least, that was the one they'd rebooked us on. Not knowing how far our gate was, or how long it would take to get there, we pressed on. My mindset is always to find where we are supposed to be, then relax and eat or shop or whatever. We discovered, as we trekked mile after mile, following the signs, we'd need to take a bus to another terminal. With no seats available, we hung onto poles inside the shuttle. Trying to keep our balance over bumpy roads, I thought about how long we'd have to wait, considering the time now. *Oh boy! We'll have an eight-hour wait here! Arg! Lord, what good can You make out of this?* I grumbled. Sighing, I noticed that the couple, who sat across from us in the Minneapolis airport holding hands, were also on the bus, and they had familiar tags on their bags. *They must be on the same trip as we are!* I thought. As we exited the vehicle, I turned to the wife and asked if they were with our company.

"Yes!" she responded. We eagerly shared information about where we were from and the ordeals of our flight to Paris. Lori and Mike were from Wisconsin.

Inside the terminal, I was pleasantly surprised to find a large seating area with plenty of comfortable couches, chairs, and tables. Restrooms and a café were conveniently along one side. Apparently, they expected travelers through Paris to have extended wait times for their connecting flights! We found a long couch with plugs for our phones and Kindles, and I was able to lean my head back over the top of the cushiony seat and catch up on some sleep. After a while, we realized we were hungry, and I walked over to the café, where I found Lori. I invited them to eat with us, but they'd chowed down earlier.

"We didn't care for the food on the plane," she explained, understandably, "and we were starving!"

We ended up with surprisingly-good chicken salad, bread, quiche, and fruit. I considered the quality way better than the premade, shrink-wrapped stuff in American airports. Later, Lori came over to the cushy couch, where we'd resumed our catnaps, and said they'd like to join us, so we offered to sit with them at their table. The ensuing conversation was inspiring to the point that Lori announced, "Our meeting was no coincidence!" I agreed.

Her husband was also in the process of retiring, and this was one of his last trips. Like us, they were passionate about mentoring and discipling. I talked about my burgeoning single moms' group and a men's breakfast that my husband attended every week. Currently, they were young-adult group leaders in their church. But their dream was to help young couples survive the ordeals of marriage, and they wanted to start a group especially for newly-weds. They were currently searching for ways to do this. She saw one open door through a friend, who offered to host the group, but she wasn't sure if she should proceed.

"What if no one comes?" she wondered out loud.

I thought of the quote in the famous 1989 movie, *Field of Dreams*: "If you build it, they will come." And I had some inspired advice for her.

"God put this desire on your heart!" I said excitedly. "He'll show you how to achieve it. Sounds like He's already making a way. Take this first step—the invitation from a friend to host your group—then He'll open more doors. It's always one step at a time." *They will come!* I thought.

Lori nodded. And I prayed for their dream.

"Lord, help them find their way to this wonderful aspiration!"

In every trip, we experienced "God winks," where He placed us in front of people to speak into their lives through prayer. I realized now that this encounter might just be the reason for this trip! Looking back, I believe it was.

Lori and Mike had come a week early to spend time with friends in Spain, touring through towns they wouldn't get to see while attending the company-sponsored, week-long Costa del Sol stay. Each week, our company hosted a new group of around sixty people at the Puente Romano Resort, where we were staying. Lori and Mike would attend the week after us. So, we wouldn't be on the same tours or at the same meetings. But I determined, I'd stay in touch with her, and I hoped that, one day, we'd see them again.

In a groggy haze, lulled by the humming sound of the plane engine, I felt like I was dreaming as we flew south from Paris over France and Spain. Through the window, I looked out at large patches of green and small dark squares and triangles where towns lay. These morphed into irregular shapes of different shades of green, sometimes lighter or darker, where trees grew. Serpentine thinning and thickening lines wound through them, where rivers cut into the patches. Small dots and large blue blobs broke up the landscape where lakes sprang up. Farther off, I could see a jagged coastline and islands set like gems in a dazzling sea. I realized I was catching glimpses of Bordeaux and Biarritz—places I'd visited in France. But mostly, all I could see was a coastline edged with thin strips of creamy sand, and, beyond that, a momentous mass of sun-reflecting turquoise. *Breathtaking!*

Trying to snap out of my dazed, almost drugged-like state, I sipped a much-needed cup of creamy coffee and breathed in the sweet smell of served pastries. Still in a semi-stupor, I was mesmerized by the clouds in so many shapes and sizes out my window: puffs, slabs, cotton balls, hilly and meadow-like wisps. Between the shapes, I spotted mountains, a large lake, and more squarish, multicolored patches. *Was I dreaming?* I wasn't sure since I'd been traveling without sleep for about twenty-four hours!

The clouds outside my window

At the Málaga airport, we met up with Lori and Mike at the baggage carousel, and I hugged Lori.

"Let's stay in touch!" I said enthusiastically.

"Yes!" she responded. "It was absolutely no coincidence that we met!"

I nodded. She smiled as we headed off with our luggage in tow.

My phone buzzed and a representative from the travel company used for our trip was on the line. Mary Claire had called us in the Paris airport, and I'd filled her in on our delay getting out. Now, she checked in to let us know that someone was waiting for us outside. I was grateful that she was making sure we got to our destination. It'd been a very long "day." A suited man was waiting for us in the parking lot. He graciously opened our doors, tossed our luggage in the back, and drove us to the resort in his big black six-seater car. It was about an hour away, and the scenery consisted of sparsely-vegetated hills, some populated with thickly-treed avocado and mango farms. Our driver pointed out many high-rise apartments along the coast to accommodate all the people drawn to this sunny area. Between the buildings, I caught flashing scenes of a palm-tree-lined beach. He noted proudly that there are 320 days of sunshine in this area of southern Spain.

"That's why so many people come here to live or spend their vacation!" He nodded back to us. Then he admitted that he loved it so much that he'd relocated his entire family from Venezuela to enjoy the relaxed and pleasant lifestyle. Though I was sure the cost of living was a great deal more here, I could understand his desire to have family close, considering the challenges of living in Venezuela.

After winding through the palm-treed streets of Marbella and hearing about the famous people who lived there, including Sean Connery, we pulled into the resort entrance. As our driver unloaded our luggage, we thanked him profusely for a safe and informative ride. In the lobby, we were greeted by staff, served sparkling water, and told we must wait for our room to be made ready. It was 9:00 pm; I was exhausted and surprised by the delay. After sitting for about thirty minutes, I asked one of the receptionists if the room might be ready yet, and she hurriedly went to find out and came back. A man with a British accent came bounding up to load us onto a golf cart then zipped us away to our room. He unlocked an outdoor gate and ushered us up three flights of tiled steps to the top floor. Huffing and puffing, I turned to Mike and asked, "Will this be a problem for you?" He shook his head. I let out a breath, and we continued the ascent. I was thankful we weren't lugging our bags up these steps, since they were delivered.

The cheerful Englishman unlocked our door and swept his arm toward the room, smiling, like he was ushering us into the grand suite of Buckingham Palace. He walked over and threw back floor to ceiling curtains, and I glided past our luggage, already set on stands by the bed, toward the sliding-glass door. I gasped as I gazed out at a deck with a glorious view of tiled rooftops backset by a setting sun, and I decided I could live with this! Extraordinarily nice, the room boasted a king-size bed, contemporary desk and drawers, and an L-shaped couch around an oval coffee table. The enclosed deck held a white table with two chairs inviting us outside, and I decided right then, *That is where I want to be!*

We thanked the accommodating man, and he left us with a swirl of welcoming words.

The view from our balcony

It was now 10 pm, and we were starving. We'd had nothing to eat since lunch in the Paris airport. I showered quickly to remove the grungy, travel-grit feeling and changed into nicer clothes. We headed downstairs and descended into lamplit darkness. Around a corner, we checked out the on-site restaurants, which were thankfully still open. A courtyard table in front of El Pimpi Restaurant beckoned to us, and a waiter welcomed us warmly, inviting us to sit down and order. Greeted by the warm glow of a table-lamp, a bottle of sparkling water, and glasses of a local red wine, we were in heaven. Our waiter, Roberto, dressed in a crisp-white, buttoned-up jacket, suggested a grilled turbot with avocado salad. We took him up on this suggestion and ordered grilled veggies on the side.

Delicious fish at El Pimpi

We could smell the mouth-watering fragrance of the pan-seared fish before it even arrived. But it was mostly Roberto's impressive demonstration and attention to detail that made it worth the wait to be here. With a swooping gesture, he brought out a sizzling pan of golden, crusty-brown turbot. On a table beside us, he waved two utensils gracefully like orchestral batons to lift each half onto our dishes, making sure he picked up every crumb. Then he dove into the vegetables with a large spoon and artfully placed them to the side of the enticing fish, creating colorful bouquets of broccoli, carrots, and cauliflower. We were starving, but we didn't want to inhale what lay beautifully-prepared on our plates, so we carefully lifted each bite of fish or vegetable up to our lips so we could savor each satisfying bite. And, with each new flavor, the feeling of fatigue seemed to melt away.

Though we should have been exhausted, we were enlivened by the wonderful ambiance and warmth of this marvelous place. I thought of how, if we'd eaten a similar meal on our deck at home, it would have been nice. But, here, surrounded by palm trees and whitewashed, red-tiled buildings, listening to Spanish music, and watching as elegantly-dressed ladies walked by in long, beautiful dresses, what might have been just another wonderful meal became an other-worldly experience. Somehow, the food and wine tasted so much better! It always seemed to be this way when we traveled. I couldn't explain it, but everything was always so much more extraordinary!

Finally, in bed by midnight, we wondered what the rest of this week would look like. What other surprising and unexpected occurrences would we experience? We couldn't imagine, since this was just our first day! A long day, granted, filled with a litany of surprising challenges and changes. But we'd made it. And we'd just experienced an amazing meal that more than made up for the tedious discomforts and delays.

For these things, we were extremely thankful!

## Chapter Two
# Magical Mijas

"It's time to get up!" I heard a breathy whisper, and my eyes popped open. Mike pointed to his watch. It was 9:00 o'clock in the morning. I wasn't surprised, since my sleep was sporadic, and I was so exhausted from the day before. It occurred to me, at that moment, I'd missed the company-required meeting at 8:30. *They'll have to understand,* I thought then smiled to myself. *What's the worst thing they can do to me?* I laughed out loud. *Fire me?* This was especially humorous, considering that I'd started my retirement transition three years before and this was my last company-sponsored trip. *Ha ha!* Besides, the things they'd share at the meeting: how the company was doing, what products and services were now available, new insights and ways of working…I would need none of these now! I hadn't stepped into my office for two and a half years, having transferred all my clients to three wonderful, capable women!

I leisurely got out of bed, showered, dressed, then sighed as I wrestled with the Nespresso coffeemaker, craving a cup of steaming hot coffee. I've found, in Europe, that many places offer guests the magnanimous feature of a fancy coffeemaker in their room. I very much appreciate the thoughtfulness of the gesture, but I've grown to resent the hassle of trying to figure out each one, because they all come with their own set of rules. This was no exception! We needed a manual to decipher how to work it. Unfortunately, there was none available. Finally, after many attempts, we somehow landed on the right combination of lifting and lowering the lid, punching certain buttons at the right time, and *voila!* It worked!

"Thank You, God!" I muttered.

After slugging down two strong cups, I set out to trek down the multi-level steps to the gate entrance, with Mike teetering on stiff legs behind me. Turning left, we drifted, mesmerized, over beautiful, plant-lined brick paths, past arched Spanish-styled doorways, and over quaint wooden bridges. We gazed up at unusual, colorfully-flowered trees as we made our way to breakfast at the Sea Grill. Drifting trance-like through this dreamy promenade, we were lulled by the captivating scenery, especially after two days of sleep deprivation.

Our walk to the Sea Grill

We found the restaurant and a small table inside with a beautiful view of a palm trees and a beach. Up a few steps, we spotted a long table loaded with every kind of cheese imaginable. That alone made my head explode with delight. But other tables held many-flavored yoghurts, breads galore, luscious and savory juices and fruits, and multiple varieties of sliced meats. I was in heaven, and I knew Mike was too! Without question, this was his favorite part of any overseas excursion—a lavish and inviting breakfast buffet!

On these amazing tours, the breakfast smorgasbords were always endless—with all manner of choices and often a made-to-order omelet bar. We'd found, with every trip to Europe, morning meals always included delicacies Americans might save for lunch, like sliced meats, cheeses, and different kinds of breads. Lunches and dinners, often on our own, were never a disappointment either, no matter what country we were visiting. This trip would be no exception.

The breakfast buffet

A welcoming waiter brought us our own carafe of coffee, and I sighed contentedly, especially after taking my first sip of the strong European blend. The smell alone charged my senses. Then I noticed another couple from our company wearing nametags and sitting at a table nearby. *I guess I'm not the only one missing our "mandatory" meeting,* I thought, feeling somewhat relieved. Coffee in hand, I stared at the small glasses of celery and carrot juice lined up in front of me, thinking how unusual these flavors would taste compared to what I usually drank for breakfast—plain orange juice. Beside these, a colorful bowl of yoghurt and a plated slice of brown banana-bread sat invitingly. Taking my time to appreciate each bite, I savored the creamy yoghurt mixed with sweet blueberries and tart blackberries. The varied flavors awakened my tastebuds even more and confirmed that I was in heaven.

I watched Mike make trip after trip from our table to the buffet, making sure he hadn't missed anything. I was particularly enthralled with his avocado open-faced sandwich—a thick piece of brown bread loaded with mashed avocado and topped with sour cream sprinkled with herbs and carrot zests. He also partook of almost every kind of fruit, yoghurt, juice, and a variety of cheese and meat. There was no way I could eat that much!

Seeing my reflection in the sunlit window next to us, my thoughts quickly turned to my suffering eye. Sadly, it was still swollen, puffy, itchy, and red. I decided, after breakfast, to go to the lobby and ask if a doctor could see me that day. *Surely, they have someone who can come and look at it,* I thought, wondering what the doctors in Spain were like, and which ones would be willing to come to resorts or hotels to see patients. An attendant in the reception area was very helpful, and he arranged for Dr. Cano to come to our room at 12:20 pm. It was 11:00 now.

Since Mike couldn't find the sunglasses he thought he'd brought with him, we set out for the onsite gift shop, where they sold all kinds of necessary paraphernalia. Through a maze of other-worldly fauna, we found The Boutique and two lovely young women inside—Luna from

Spain and Tilda from Sweden. I asked if they had any sunglasses, and they pointed to a shelf. As Mike tried on several pairs, I attempted to make conversation. Somehow the subject of the Camino de Santiago came up, when I asked where they were from, and I told them about my journey and why I'd decided to do the pilgrimage in honor of my deceased son. Both were interested and talked about wanting to do it, so I showed them a picture of the book I'd written about my adventure, *The Camino Connection*. It was a sweet and meaningful encounter for me. Hopefully it was for them too.

Back in our room, Dr. Cano knocked promptly at 12:20 and asked which of us was the patient. I showed him my swollen eye, and he immediately set about writing me a prescription for special eye drops and a salve, which I'd need to get at a pharmacy. We were going to a nearby town that day, and I could get them then. I was impressed by the doctor's ability to so quickly diagnose my problem and come up with a solution. I wondered if all Spanish doctors are trained to treat any issue, including those concerning the eyes. In the States, doctors are mostly specialized and treat only problems relating to their area of expertise. For eyes, I would have to go to an optometrist or ophthalmologist. So, I was surprised by this doctor's broad range of knowledge.

Dr. Cano also suggested something I didn't expect. He said, "Take a chamomile tea bag, after soaking it in water, and press it against your eye. This will help your eye heal faster. It's a natural anti-inflammatory." I had never heard of this. Again, I wondered if Spanish doctors are trained on using natural remedies. *Wow!* I thought. *I wish more doctors would disseminate information like this, instead of prescribing expensive drugs for every ailment.*

In a special room off the path that led to El Pimpi Restaurant, we met up with others from my company. They stood around tables covered with maps and pamphlets, checking out information about local towns and venues. About fifty of us geared up for a tour that afternoon of Mijas, a picturesque Andalusian village of about 90,000 set on the side of a mountain about forty-five minutes away.

On the bus, I read a brochure description of Mijas: "Traverse the labyrinthine network of narrow streets and ascend the steep lanes adorned with whitewashed houses and iron-grilled windows, immersing yourself in the enchanting ambiance of this coastal paradise. You'll also see the Plaza de Toros, the smallest bullring in Spain, with its collection of colorfully adorned matador costumes and vintage posters from bullfights of the past."

This all sounded amazing! But, as it turned out, my favorite sight in Mijas was the burros lined up for rides, with carts sometimes hitched to their backs. They hearkened back to a time when this was the main form of transportation for tourists. I thought the burros were amusing and endearing.

A reminder of Mijas's burros

A famous chapel sat on a hilltop in Mijas. Named Ermita de la Virgen de la Pēna, or Hermitage of the Virgin of the Rock, it was excavated from the side of a hill around 1548 by friars from the Order of the Blessed Virgin Mary of Mercy. A Catholic order founded in 1218, its members were known for offering their lives for others in danger of losing their faith. The site commemorated Marian apparitions that began in 1586, when two children, Juan and Asuncion Bernal Linaire, had a vision of Mary. It reminded me of similar incidents where children saw Jesus's mother, one near Fatima, Portugal. When I mentioned this to our guide, she responded, "Yes. There have been hundreds of Mary sightings in Europe!"

Beside the chapel, I was greeted by a statue of Jesus, gazing warmly down at me from a huge rock. He pointed to his heart that was bound by a crown of thorns and emanated flames. These symbols were to remind people of his suffering, his love for humanity, and the transformative power of his love, according to *Catholic Answers*.

Hermitage of the Virgin of the Rock

Rising behind the arched chapel entryway, a stone-built belltower summoned worshippers to prayer. Inside the tiny chapel, unlit candles sat symbolically on two tables with a silver-handled vase of white flowers. Behind these, a glowing statue of Mary embraced a crowned baby while standing on a half-moon. This reminded me of the Bible verse in Revelation 12:1: "And a great sign appeared in heaven: a woman clothed with the sun, with the moon under her feet, and on her head a crown of twelve stars."

Back outside, I looked up again at the statue of Jesus and thought about his heart-reminders—how He gave up His own life so others could live. I admired Mary and her willingness to serve God by having this incredible child. Her gift to us was great, because of her willingness to suffer at the hands of others before her son's birth, during his life, and at his death. But she would be the first to say that she didn't do this so we would worship her. No! She listened and obeyed God so we could, through her son, know and worship Him in a much greater way. She understood the goodness, lovingkindness, and holiness of a God worthy of our praise!

Past the statue, a walkway led behind the chapel and offered a beautiful view of the valley below. This was a favorite scene at the site.

We walked up the street to Carromato—an exhibit of miniature art, then on to a circular fountain standing prominently in the middle of a plaza. From this focal-point, a brick-paved street wound uphill, past many white-washed buildings. We wandered down another street lined with colorful chairs and small round tables that invited tourists to sit for a while and enjoy another wonderful scene. Our guide pointed to a long, white-washed building decorated with many blue pots of red geraniums. Many from our group stood still, gawking at the flowers and breathing in the rosy scent. The almost-citrusy aroma made us feel clean and uplifted, even as we trekked and sweated, going uphill.

It reminded me of a bright red house with a tiled roof near Logroño, Spain, on the Camino trail. The building stood out because the tall iron fence in front of it was so abundantly decorated with hundreds of colorful pots filled with flowers. Not just blue-hued, the containers were yellow, green, clay-colored, and white. They held not only geraniums but daisies, lilies, petunias, and marigolds. It was a glorious sight and not one I'll ever forget.

The blue-potted building

Walking away from the bright-blue-potted display, we gazed through several arches and were entranced by a hill covered with red-tiled, white-washed houses that stair-stepped up toward the top. The view reminded me of one of my favorite places on earth—Santorini Island in Greece. In case you've never been to this awe-inspiring place, let me try to describe it. Close your eyes and imagine sparkling, white-washed, blue-tile-roofed buildings sitting hundreds of feet up, atop the cratered edge of a submerged volcano that jutted up from the Mediterranean Sea. The island reminded me of blue French-tipped nails on the fingers of a hand reaching up from the ocean. It was breathtaking, especially when you sat in a café high up, inside one of the dazzling buildings. Sipping a cappuccino, you gazed down as ship after ship furled through the sea-filled crater toward the landing far below.

Not quite as spectacular, these hillside homes were still dramatic and captivating.

Sadly, Plaza de Toros, the smallest bullring in Spain, was closed that day, so we peeked through an arched, gated doorway at a collection of matador costumes and bullfighting posters. We tried to envision what it would be like to sit inside the ring, surrounded by crowds. Yelling hurrahs for the matador to succeed at lancing his ferocious aggressor, we could smell and taste the fear. We'd scream our heads off when he was almost pinned by the bull's piercing horns as he waved his red cape to tease the animal into even more violent behavior. I'd never been to a bullfight, but I could imagine it.

Bullfighting is a treasured blood-sport tradition in Spain, and I respect and appreciate the Spanish passion, however different from my own. I have no pressing feelings pro or con regarding it, but I wondered how it might feel to watch the treatment of the animals involved. To see the bulls being lanced might make me very sad. I had also read about horses being gored during bullfights. It would also be upsetting to see a matador on foot or a picador on a horse hurt during a performance, but I thought, *They did choose to do this!* Not so much the bull or the horse.

Our town-tour ended with time on our own, and I looked around for a pharmacy to purchase my eye medication. I quickly realized that most of the drugstores were shut down for the afternoon. This is typical for Spain. I experienced unexpected hours of operation while journeying through the Camino. When I entered a town, looking for a pharmacy to buy more tape to bandage my blistered feet, I often discovered they were all closed for the day, not to reopen until the evening. I expressed my need for fulfilling my prescription to our guide; she kindly found one that was open 24/7 and offered to walk me there. We approached and noticed that it was gated shut. She rang a doorbell, and a man came zipping up to open the door. I was thankful for her insight and relieved, since this was my only chance to get the needed eyedrops and ointment.

After this little side trek, Mike and I decided to find a place to get a drink. The midday sun was glaring down from a cloudless sky, and its rays were bouncing off the light-colored stones that paved the streets, creating a blinding and warming effect. I was sweaty and thirsty. Up one street, we noticed many empty tables under a canopy in front of one restaurant. This seemed odd since all the other outdoor cafés were crowded with people. After ordering the local recommended beverage, Tinto de Verano—a cold, wine-based drink like sangria—we soon realized why the tables here were mostly vacant. I asked a waiter if he could take our picture. His response? He shook his head with a frown and bounded inside, not choosing to return. I wondered if he didn't speak English, but I'd tried to make it easy for him by holding up my phone. Finishing my drink, I gazed around at the still-empty tables. Thankfully, a passer-by gladly took our picture.

Sipping Tinto de Veranos in Mijas

With no waiter in sight and wanting to get back to our bus in time for departure, I went inside the restaurant to pay and use the restroom. I could hear the clanking of pots and dishes from the kitchen in back, and I walked up to a counter near the door. I encountered two waitstaff, who avoided eye contact and continued to talk. I found the facilities on my own. *Not a very friendly or welcoming place,* I decided, brushing past them. Before going back outside, I again approached the two. They still ignored me. When I held out cash, they stopped talking, happy to take my money. *Hmmm. Maybe they just don't like tourists here.*

I'd heard about recent organized protests in cities like Barcelona, where locals expressed frustration over tourism. Understandably, they disliked the impacts to their quality of life from overcrowding, including strains on resources and the growing lack of affordable housing due to the influx of outsiders. I wondered about smaller towns like Mijas. *Did they also feel burdened by visitors?*

On our way back to the bus, I took a picture of a white marble statue depicting a man loaded with heavy rope-tied bags. It made me feel weighted down, and I wondered who it was and what it meant. I read that it commemorated the Esparto—workers who once hauled loads of grass to town for making ropes, mats, baskets, and stucco. Now, the villagers, instead of bearing ponderous grass-bags uphill to carry on their livelihoods, must endure a different kind of upheaval. They watch as tourists pour from busses into their peaceful existence to crowd through the narrow streets and view life in their quaint, historically preserved pueblos. *Change always seems to bring disruption*, I thought. And I felt at once happy for the villagers—that they no longer had to bear these heavy loads uphill to survive. But I also empathized with how they must dislike and resent the people who disrupt their lives every day.

The statue of an Esparto

After a forty-five-minute ride back to Puente Romano, I spoke to a local lady at the information tables about other towns we could visit on our one free day. The short, dark-haired, older Spanish woman, hired by our company to answer questions about local points of interest, tried to be helpful. She grabbed a map from one table and unfolded it dramatically. Since we wanted to experience the town of Cordoba, she pointed at its location compared to where we were, and she emphasized the distance—over 131 miles away. Then she said that to hire a guide and a driver would cost us 2,110 euros or $2,472—way more than we wanted to spend for a two-hour tour and a ride to get us there and back. We asked her about another closer town—Estepona—and, after she saw my reaction to the price of venturing into Cordoba, she nodded and agreed that this would be, for us, a better option. I took the map and thought of it as a possibility.

In the lobby, I tried to make reservations at Bibo, an on-site Spanish restaurant, but the man at the desk hadn't heard of it, even though it was advertised in their brochure and on the signs along their walkways. I figured out that it was now called El Pimpi, where we'd eaten the first night. So, I made reservations at Gaia, an onsite restaurant that specializes in Mediterranean cuisine.

After a pleasant afternoon on our balcony, taking pictures of the tile roofs, alleyways, and courtyard below our room in the changing afternoon light, we walked to Gaia. We were heartily greeted by two girls, beautifully adorned in long white gowns, and waiters dressed smartly in crisp white shirts and black pants. We sat at a table for two outdoors, enjoying the ambient light from a small lamp and the scent of fresh flowers, while groups gathered at larger round tables nearby. After being served glasses of sparkling water and a local wine recommended by our sommelier, Napoleon, another waiter carefully placed my purse on a stool next to me. "Wow! I'm impressed!" I said, feeling spoiled.

We were presented first with a plate of sautéed eggplant slices, and I found each melt-in-your-mouth bite better than I could have imagined. They tasted both salty and sweet with a hint of garlic and herbs. Their consistency was soft, but not mushy, like tenderly-cooked mushrooms. The eggplant pieces were surrounded by small, sweet cherry tomatoes, buttery black olives, and a dollop of tangy creamed cheese.

We decided to be adventurous and, besides roasted chicken, ordered truffle pasta to share. The chicken was seeped in a savory sauce, and we breathed in the herby fragrance that wafted up from our plates. But we especially appreciated the perfectly-seasoned pasta, since both of us are huge truffle fans—so much so that we use truffle salt on our popcorn. Every bite and breath reminded us why we love the earthy, unique aroma and flavor of truffles.

The food was amazing, but what we loved most about Gaia was the attentiveness of the waiters. Trying to make conversation with them, I asked Napoleon about his background. From Argentina, he briefly described his passage here, avoiding the reason why he'd made the move.

I had a feeling it had to do with a lover, but I didn't want to press him to find out. I was deeply impressed by his courage. Like others I'd met here, he'd transferred to a place far from home, not knowing what to expect. I wondered how appealing the staff benefits were at this resort, and I thought, *They must make it very worthwhile to be able to attract so many talented people from all over the world.*

Somehow, our conversation turned to the topic of the Camino. Are you surprised? Mike brought it up this time!

"My wife walked on the Camino!" he announced.

"Really?" Napoleon responded. "I've thought about doing it."

"You should!" I exclaimed. "It will change your life!"

I filled him in on my own experience and encouraged him to take the plunge and create his own amazing adventure. I hope he does.

Before crashing that night, we oohed and ahhed over the amazing sunset views from our balcony, and we were grateful for a fulfilling day, despite missing out on the morning meeting. *Too bad!* I reflected, not feeling bad at all.

Thankfully, we got a decent night's sleep that night to make up for the last two days. But nothing could prepare us for what would transpire the next morning.

# HOW A GOOF BECAME A GIFT

Remarkably, we were up at 6:30 am to greet the new day. And that proved to be the best part of that morning! We had to leave at 7:30 for a tour of the Rock of Gibraltar, so we hurried to get dressed and be on our way to meet the group. Sadly, we'd miss Mike's breakfast delights in the Sea Grill, since it didn't open until 7:30. But, when we joined the others, we were provided with boxed breakfasts that included fruit, cookies, biscuits, cheese, crackers, drinks, and more than we could possibly consume at one sitting. We ate a few bites, downed as much coffee as we could, and left the rest for the staff.

Herded onto a bus, we sat near the middle, and I chose a window seat on the driver side, facing the front, forgetting that I was beside Mike's near-deaf ear. His cochlear implant, providing much better hearing, was on his right side. Our guide, David, welcomed the thirty or so of us and, as we drove through Marbella, well on our way from the resort, he proceeded to explain where we were going and what we would see. The tour would take us to the summit of Gibraltar, where, according to our brochure, we would behold "a spectacular view of the Spanish mainland with the snowcapped Sierra Nevada in the distance and the blue Mediterranean waters of the Costa del Sol in the foreground." With the coast of Africa within view, we'd also see the famous apes that had free range of the "Apes' Den."

Then, David made a life-altering announcement.

"Everyone has their passport! *Right?*" he exclaimed, leaving no question as to whether they were necessary. "You *will* need them to get into Gibraltar, since it's a British territory."

The moment he uttered these words, I felt beads of sweat forming on my brow, because I knew I'd overlooked this minor detail when packing my purse full of items we might need for this day-long tour. For whatever reason, I'd forgotten the most important thing. Now, I blame it on jet lag and not being present for the company meeting, where they reminded everyone on this excursion to bring their passports. I'd also failed to reread the brochure about the tour. After this, I was intent on reading *all* the details for the remaining tours.

Now, I dug through my bag, knowing they weren't there, but hoping they'd miraculously appear. Finding my search fruitless, as I knew I would, I wasn't about to announce to the group that we didn't have ours and make the bus turn around. It was too late for that. My heart pounded furiously. I muttered and felt like I might have a heart attack as I searched my mind for what we could do to avoid a complete catastrophe. I remembered taking photos of the identifying pages in our passports, so I scrolled frantically through my phone. But I couldn't find them. *I must have deleted them,* I sighed. *Fantastic!* I did find our passport numbers in my phone notes, and I wondered if these and our drivers' licenses would suffice. I'd just have to ask. In the meantime, my mind raced through all the possibilities, and, as moisture built up on my forehead and in my eyes, dribbling down both cheeks, I prayed, *Lord, would You perform some sort of miracle here?*

Then, I thought, I needed to let Mike know. *Arg!*

At that moment, I heard exaggerated munching and smelled the cheddary odor of cheese. And I knew at least one person on the bus was awake, and it happened to be someone right in front of us. I was unwilling to let him and everyone else on the bus hear about my predicament and wonder what kind of stupidity would cause someone to have such a terrible brain lapse. So, in my hoarsest, most anxiety-ridden voice, I whispered, "I didn't bring our passports." Mike's answer? *"Wha-a-at? I can't hear you!"*

I raised my voice, still trying to stay under the radar.

"Our passports. I don't have them!"

*"I still can't hear you!"* he boomed.

*"Never mind!"*

I faced the window, my heart pounding like mad, while Mike leaned back in his chair, trying to enjoy yet another snooze. Wondering what we might miss at this famous site, I tried to poopoo the tour. I remembered what a friend had told me before we left. "The Rock tour isn't all that great!" she said. Sarcastically, I said to myself, *Yea, it probably isn't at all what it's cracked up to be!* But then I opened my brochure, and I sighed as I read, "the nearly 1,400-foot-high rock of Gibraltar towers over the Mediterranean at the point where Europe ends…. The Romans…believed it to be one of the Pillars of Hercules standing at the entrance to the sea. For centuries, Gibraltar was strategically important and was at various times part of the Moorish, Spanish, British and Dutch empires. Captured by the British Fleet in 1704…, it was ceded to Britain in 1713 and has remained under British control since, although it is now a UK Overseas Territory with its own government."

"Dang!" I groused. "We might miss this!"

We reached the parking lot to the entrance of Gibraltar, and, after stepping off the bus, I ran over to David to make my sad confession.

"I forgot our passports," I muttered, barely audible.

David stared at me and furrowed his brows.

*Not a good sign,* I thought.

"I have the passport numbers and our drivers' licenses!" I said hopefully, my voice pleading.

"I have never heard of them letting *anyone* through without passports," David admitted sadly, "but I'll check with the other guides and get their input."

While he called, my heart thumped against my chest, and I stood there, my hands shaking. Another guide came up, and I told her what had transpired. Lany had the same unsettling look of concern as David, who stepped back up to us.

"They're saying that you might be able to get in, but they might not let you back out." He grimaced.

"Well, *that's a problem!*" I sighed. "I don't want to take that chance!"

Lany nodded. But she had an idea. She pointed out the taxi-stand and where to get coffee nearby.

"There really isn't anything much to see in this area," she explained. "But you could take a taxi to Estepona, where there's more to do and see."

"We'll think about it." I took a deep breath, wondering what our best alternative was. "I think we'll get some coffee and talk about it."

"I'll check back with you to see what you decided to do," Lany promised, and I appreciated her concern for us.

The Rock of Gibraltar from a distance

The guides were understanding, but there was nothing more they could do. I realized this, and we turned to walk across the street to check out the local cafés. My first order of business was finding a restroom. At one café on a walkway lined with small eateries, I walked up to a woman smoking under a canopy, and I asked where the closest facility was. She got up, snuffed out her cigarette in an ashtray, went over to the café counter to retrieve a key, then walked me up the alley to a public restroom. She unlocked a large metal door, and I thanked her profusely.

One of my frequent prayers is, *Lord, if there's something I need to do, please remind me if I've forgotten about it!* I wondered now why He hadn't jogged my memory about the passports, or poked me a few times, as He usually does. Inside the public restroom, grateful for this godsend, I wondered if God knew I'd need a toilet at that moment—something I wouldn't have had on the tour—and this was one reason for my forgetfulness about our passports.

After using the facility, I joined Mike, and we traipsed back to the same café to order coffee, wanting to give them our business, since the lady there was kind enough to help us. As we sipped cappuccinos, we talked about whether we'd stay here and read until our group returned to the bus at 1:30 for the ride back or take a cab to Estepona—between Gibraltar and the resort. We'd have to cab-it back to Puente Romano on our own and make sure we made it in time for the dinner banquet. It was 9:30 now, and we weren't keen on sitting in a café for four hours. So, we decided on the taxi-ride to Estepona. Back across the street, I snapped two memorable pictures, one of The Rock from a distance and one of a statue of a man with a bicycle.

Statue of a worker in Gibraltar

Called Los Trabajadores Espanoles en Gibraltar, or "The honored Spanish workers in Gibraltar," the man in the statue reminded me of our situation—subject to the laws and needing to show a permit or visa to go in and out of Gibraltar. I felt compassion for him and others, who may have been kept from a job or an occasion because they didn't have the right permit with them! Like us!

Approaching the taxi-stand, I detected the stale smell of gasoline and cigarette smoke. A group of men huddled and puffed away under an awning, where a row of parked, marked taxis stood waiting. One man stamped out his cigarette quickly, stepped up to us, and pointed to his car. We said, "Estepona," and he nodded. Driving for about twenty-five minutes, we passed the same brown, sparsely-vegetated hills that we'd encountered on the way to Gibraltar. And I was reminded of my stressful sweating on the way to the Rock.

Located in the province of Málaga in Costa del Sol, Estepona is known for its beaches lined with tapas bars and restaurants. Entering the town of about 67,000 people, we drove along a wide, palm-lined street. With many shops and picturesque squares, it was once considered by Walt Disney Company as a site for its Eurodisney project—later awarded to Paris. Our driver pulled over near the beach. We didn't see any streets with attractive shops, so we headed toward a promenade by the ocean.

After a few steps along a wooden walkway, we sat down on a bench to get our bearings, and I searched my phone for things to do. The first attractions to pop up were boat rides into the bay that included dolphin sightings. I looked for sailboat excursions, thinking Mike would enjoy that, and I found one nearby. We set out, using my phone for directions, and we ended up on a parallel side street, passing a wedding party headed for a chapel. Little girls dressed up in white frilly dresses with matching mary-jane shoes and purses paraded past us. Oohing and aahing, I smiled with delight at this unusual sight. The tiny, dark-haired, ponytailed, olive-skinned cherubs looked over at me and grinned as they passed.

Heading up a hill, still following the wayward phone directions, Mike turned around and pointed out sailboats far below us. We headed back downhill and thankfully avoided a steep uphill trek. My delinquent phone now in my pocket, we found a large marina filled with boats of all shapes and sizes, and I stopped a woman on the street to ask where we could get tickets for a sailboat ride. She happily escorted us to an open-air pavilion and a sign-up stand for sailboat rides. What looked to me like an elderly Spanish man greeted us, and I realized that he was probably about our age! I reflected on the many times I'd looked over at aging individuals and thought, *Wow, that person looks old,* only to realize that they were younger than me! It was always a humbling experience.

The welcoming man looked at his afternoon schedule, and, in broken English, found an opening at 2:00 pm. *Hurray!* We jumped at this. He wanted 125 euros in payment, so I found an ATM machine close by and brought him the cash as he finished writing out a receipt for us. Since it was only 11:00, we asked if he recommended a place to sit nearby, and he walked us to a corner and pointed to the Haloman Café. It faced the marina, and we could glimpse the blue-green sea and sailboats from our table under a canopy. Too early for lunch, we ordered beer and sparkling water and breathed a sigh of relief as we enjoyed sitting and staring at people coming and going from yachts along the docks.

The time passed quickly, and we headed back to the sailboat-ride stand, and the man who attended it. He pointed to two chairs behind him, since our ride hadn't arrived yet. Finally, seeing it in the distance, he motioned toward the dock, and we followed him to watch as a vessel slowly approached. The boat pulled up to the dock, and about twenty-five young girls jumped off, singing and swaying their hips—obviously a bachelorette party. Dressed in bikinis and skimpy outfits, they giggled and chattered, their voices almost drowned out by rock music that blared from a speaker on the boat. Another girl-party standing near us on the dock joined in, and off they paraded, shrieking and screaming hilariously, with a proudly-sauced, bridal-veil-bedecked girl in the lead. The blasting music followed them off the platform as their voices trailed away down the beach.

When our boat finally glided toward the dock, and another group of about twenty women jumped off—a laughing mix of young and old. I wondered how the captain and his assistant were going to feel about transitioning from pretty, partying women to two old, somber fogies. The man from the stand approached the owner and, speaking Spanish, explained how we were his next ride. Captain Eugenio, with his young helper, Jared, cordially helped us climb onboard, making us feel even older than we were! It was a forty-eight-foot sailboat with a cabin beneath. We sat in the cockpit with the captain, who took turns piloting with Jared. Shaded by a roof, we gazed out at the water on all sides. I was surprised when we headed out to sea and never actually set sail. Instead, they used a motor for power. *Faster and easier to control the boat?* I wondered. Nonetheless, it was a pleasant hour-long excursion into the expansive bay.

Far away from the marina, we were told that dolphin sightings were very rare these days and not to expect to see any. *Hmmm.* But, somehow, I was ok with that. Just sitting in a boat, looking out at the changing scenery, as we whipped through lapis-blue water was enough for me at that moment. The sun was shining, and it was in the 70s—a perfect Fahrenheit temperature. Though my heart was heavy, and I had a knot in my stomach, still feeling somewhat disappointed at missing out on the tour, I appreciated this God-given chance to be on a boat. Especially on such a nice day with views from a seaside arena.

I always love being on the water. I enjoy moving farther and farther away from shore and feeling sea sprays as they shoot up from the boat-waves and cool my face. I like gazing back at where I've been. It reminds me of God's perspective on things—how He can look forward, or back, at a scene and get ever-changing, evolving frames of reference. I glanced toward the shore and watched buildings and people grow smaller and smaller. It made me realize how the things we think are so important at any given moment become less relevant and more meaningless the farther away we get from them. Out at sea, I can experience a completely different view of life through another, sometimes breathtaking, perspective.

I thought of summers as a young girl in Michigan and boat rides with my grandfather. Closing my eyes, I imagined my grandparents' log cabin. I breathed in the fragrant, tall pine trees that stood proudly around it, and I felt the soft, creamy sand between my toes as I approached the crisp chill of the crystalline, turquoise-tinted, spring-fed lake. I loved to sunbathe, create sandcastles, and plunge, screaming, into the frigid water to swim to a nearby anchored raft. I'd lay for hours on the wooden planks, basking in the cool breezes and cloudless sunlight, feeling a little bit of freedom from the adults who supervised from the shore. I'd breathe in the smell of Coppertone sunscreen slathered all over my body and watch the passing sailboats and speedboats with skiers in tow.

Sometimes, Grampa would take me on his yellow StarCraft fiberglass motorboat with the Evinrude 40-horsepower outboard for a sight-seeing tour around the lake. Or he'd tow me, glancing back to see if I'd managed to rise up to the surface to ski for a distance. That was when I learned how to make my way up to stand and glide over the waves, feeling the power of the boat as it pulled me by a rope. I remember saying to myself, "I will do this for Paul McCartney!"—my Beetle-idol as a young teen. Sometimes it worked. Sometimes it didn't. I learned then that idols can't always help you overcome things. From that experience, I began to realize that prayers to God were far more effective.

I especially liked cruises with my grandfather around the lake to check out other cabins, people lying on the beach, or fancy boats moored to anchors or tied to docks. When my teenage cousins visited, they'd reluctantly include my sister, brother, and me to go girl-watching. We found this very amusing and interesting as adolescents.

When I was thirteen, my mother took me, along with eight other teens and another chaperone, on an extended tour of Europe. This trip changed my life. My eyes were opened to places I'd never seen, and it made me long to return to the most scenic and memorable ones. Since it was the mid-1960s, and air travel was not quite as popular then as it is today, we traversed the Atlantic on a ship—the S.S. France. My most meaningful memory of that voyage was getting up at dawn to watch the sun rise over the ocean and feeling overwhelmed as I gazed out at the surrounding expanse of wave-rippling water on all sides. No sight of land anywhere. To me, that was spectacular!

These summertime excursions made me appreciate any kind of boat-ride, where I could feel the breezes and splashes against my face, breathe in the smell of fresh-lake or saltwater mixed with fuel and listen to the roar of an engine. I loved to watch the white-foamed water that gushed in streams behind me, creating rippling waves that spread out on all sides.

From our sailboat now on the Mediterranean Sea, I spotted the Rock of Gibraltar and Morocco facing it—far off in the distance. The scene was spectacular, and I was grateful for this unusual view. Eugenio pleasantly answered our questions about his life and background, giving us an abbreviated version of his story. While talking, he brought out a pink-colored bottle of wine—a very tasty rosé. I sipped it from a plastic wine glass and savored its unusual crispness—perfect on a sunshiny day!

After our "sailing" adventure, we walked back to the Haloman Café to see if they could summon a cab for us. The waiter who'd served us before stepped up and made a quick call. After only a few minutes, a taxi roared around the corner and pulled up to take us to Puente Romano, about twenty minutes away.

Back to our room, we rested for the remainder of the afternoon then headed to the lobby for a short bus trip with our group to a place called Cortijo de Cortés for a theme dinner. On every company trip, a very special meal is always included, where we are bussed to an off-site location. There, we're wined, dined, and entertained lavishly.

On a trip to Vienna, Austria, in 2002, we went to a small village, where we were greeted by local people dressed in traditional Austrian costumes with glasses of beer on platters. Local singers serenaded us with German songs and played accordions and guitars as we entered the town. They escorted us down into an underground cellar, where they served us more local beer and German food that covered the long tables where we sat. Then, they sang and danced for us as we ate. We were thoroughly entertained by it all.

This evening, we were greeted and led into a courtyard, where a singing group and waiters with trays full of sangria greeted us. The venue, Cortijo de Cortés, is reserved for weddings and family or corporate events.

Singers and guitarists at Cortijo de Cortés

Beside the courtyard, I was surprised to see a man and a woman on horseback, standing silently, watching us and wearing brimmed hats, gold-braided brown jackets and vests, crisp white shirts, brown pants, and high-topped brown boots. Their suede-gloved hands held the reins tightly as they posed stiffly on English saddles. The horses stood like obedient statues with their heads barely raised. Above them, winding red-rose vines shaded them with many blooms from a metal trellis, offering their sweet fragrance. And palm leaves reached out from one side to touch them with their green spiky fingers.

Within the large courtyard, high-top tables beckoned, and savory smells wafted toward us from food-covered trays held out by eager waiters. Some trays were loaded with chopped avocado and tomato-filled ceramic spoons. Others tempted us with tiny plates of tempura-fried shrimp and miniature burgers. Still others were weighed down with glasses full of white and red sangria.

We stood at a table and listened as a quartet sang Spanish songs while strumming guitars and beating rhythmically on a tambourine. After enjoying the music and tasting every possible appetizer, we were escorted into an open-air arena and seated in rows that filled three sides. Then we watched as the two riders from the courtyard performed a perfectly-synchronized riding exercise. We were especially awed when a woman appeared in the center of the arena, dressed in a long bright-red dress with red boots, twirling a beautiful, long-fringed red Mantón de Manila. As she swung the shawl and kicked up dust in an artfully-elusive dance, a caballero on a brown horse pranced around her, like a lover wooing his amour.

An artful performance

Still breath-taken from the woman's performance, we watched as four riders—two men and two women on white and brown horses—performed a quadrille. Wearing Spanish attire, they reminded me of another performance I'd seen in Slovenia years ago. Like the magnificent white Lipizzaner stallions in that arena, these horses and riders performed many of the same movements, trotting perfectly in formation.

The show was soon over, but our feelings of amazement lingered as we descended from the arena into the courtyard. We were escorted into a crystal-chandeliered, Spanish-tiled ballroom filled with white-clothed tables and fancy skirted chairs. A young couple from Idaho, sisters from Minnesota, and a mother and daughter from Wisconsin sat around us. While we conversed with the Idaho couple about jobs, life, children, etc., my senses exploded as I breathed in the spicy and sweet fragrances of a green and purple-leafed salad. Crispy-fried eggplant strips triggered unexpected sensations, along with melt-in-your-mouth hake fish with a savory cream sauce, perfectly seasoned, sautéed green and red peppers, and little apple tarts with scoops of ice cream. But the pièce de résistance was my favorite Spanish wine—a local Rioja, which complemented the food and set off even more agreeable, mouth-watering reactions.

Between each mouth-watering bite, I tried to make conversation. I found the daughter, next to me, very talkative as she described her journey through college and a goal of one day working with her mother. Her mom was more reticent at first. But, when I casually recalled a memory, it sparked something, and her eyes lit up. I shared how I came to realize that feeling like you'd achieved something in life wasn't so much about being recognized by your fellow peers as it was about developing purposeful relationships with your clients. I described my retirement party and how my customers cried because I was leaving. In that moment, I understood my most meaningful accomplishment over twenty-five years—making an impact on their lives.

Her face and demeanor suddenly changed. She'd been at the company for five years, she moaned, and she was unhappy with the progress she'd made. I told her how it took me at least five years to see a return on all my efforts. That was when I started getting really good referrals. When I shared this, she sank into her seat with a sigh of relief and smiled. That made me glad.

After a short bus-ride back to the resort, we were in bed by 11 pm. It had been another *very* long day, made up of more surprises—unexpected diversions and delights. We realized, as we reflected on the day, God's hand had been in it *all for good*! *Wow!* That was a shocker! It was just as I'd prayed!

# Chapter Four
# THE MAMA SEAGULL

I t was a "down" day. And we were thankful for it! Relieved that we had no plans, we still got up around 9:00 am. We headed to the Sea Grill for breakfast, and Mike's mouth watered in anticipation. We ran into a couple from our group I'd met in Mijas, and, as we entered the restaurant, Bill, the husband, asked if they could sit with us.

Fish under glass at the Sea Grill

51

"Of course!" I said, before Mike could answer, knowing he'd be ok with it.

Waiting to be seated, I took a picture of a glass case filled with colorful fresh fish and one lobster that was still moving!

We were directed to a table for four then made our way to the buffet tables to pick and choose whatever appealed to us that morning. I got my usual bowl of fresh fruit and yoghurt and, this time, a small glass of ginger juice. After indulging in a cup from the coffee carafe to widen my still-sleepy eyes, I reached for the juice. From the very first sip, my tongue tingled so explosively from the ginger-infused cocktail that I had to drink some water. Despite the spiciness, I continued to taste it gingerly, knowing my stomach would love it. There were so many things here that I wished we served in the States. I'd *never* seen juice like this in a restaurant before!

I reached for the coffee carafe to refill my already-empty cup, and I watched the others hobble over with plates loaded with goodies. Mike took his time choosing what amounted to a colorful plate of creative, delectable delights that included brown bread, red salmon, green avocado, multi-colored fruit, white yoghurt, orange cheese—an assortment that appealed to him.

Between tastes, we discovered that Bill was also retiring in the next year, and this was his last company-sponsored trip. I wondered if he felt the same mixture of relief and regret as I did, knowing these were his last moments surrounded by people he might never see again. He mostly expressed regrets, and he complained about many disappointing challenges he'd faced with clients and family. He and his wife *were* proud of one daughter, who'd successfully taken over many of Bill's clients and seemed to be doing well in her new role.

After eating and comparing notes on our retirement plans, Mike and I were ready to leave these new friends. We sauntered back to our room around 12:20 pm to enjoy some quiet time on our balcony. Thinking we might luxuriate in some solitude, I experienced something far from it. After sitting for a while, appreciating the peaceful, sunny ambiance of our rooftop view, I happened to spot something unusual. When I gazed over at the white-washed building across the way, my eyes suddenly caught an unexpected movement. There…next to the building's chimney…another motion. It came from a small, white, huddled form. Now, I could see a white profile that contrasted with the red and orange tiles. Definitely a seagull, I decided. Just then, the bird flapped its wings and stood up. And I realized, she was standing over a nest! She turned toward me, cawed loudly, looked around, then settled back down on her roost. She faced me, like she was checking me out and making sure I wouldn't come over to steal her babies. I watched her for a while, interested to see her response to other gulls, who swooped around her teasingly then landed on another roof beside me. She became so preoccupied and annoyed with the rowdy bunch that she left her nest to fly over to the other rooftop and squawk at them. It was like she was carping, "Quit bothering me, you rabblerousers! You're being way to loud! You're disturbing my chicks!" Then she flew right back to her nest to tend to her eggs. She stood and faced me again, as if to say, "Not you too! You better not disturb us!"

I especially enjoyed watching Mama Seagull, since we don't live near the ocean and rarely see this bird species. Later, I discovered a bit more about why she was so cautious and defensive about the other close-flying gulls. Apparently, these birds are very predatory. They have no qualms about stealing each other's eggs. They even work in teams, with some causing a distraction, while others conduct the surreptitious egg-theft.

While gazing at her and the neighboring gulls, I thought about all the bird adventures we've had at home. One spring, a Blue Jay decided to build an elaborate nest in a pear tree next to our floor-to-ceiling kitchen window. Mike and I checked out her progress every day during our meals. She worked laboriously, because she wanted it just right for her babies. She snatched twigs, leaves, ribbons, and pieces of plastic to line the lair. When she was finished, she stood over it proudly, thinking it was beautiful! Just right for her awaiting family. Then she laid her eggs and squirmed until she sat comfortably to warm them. She nested there—morning, noon, and night, with few breaks in between. Surprisingly, her male partner brought her food, so she could stay in position. We enjoyed watching her for over two weeks, wondering when her eggs would hatch. Finally, one day, we saw tiny beaks poking up and yawning for the male bird to feed them.

"How sweet!" I thought, and I wondered how many bird species involve the male to this degree. I'd never been overly impressed with Blue Jays before, because their caw is loud, sharp, and obnoxious, but this made me feel endeared to them.

We watched for a day or two as the hatchlings stretched their necks up more and more. Then, one night, a robust storm hit our area. We could hear the wind wildly blowing through the trees in our yard, and I worried about our jay family and what might become of the babies. The next morning, I rushed to the window, concerned for what I might see. Sure enough, the nest and all its inhabitants were gone. I walked among the hostas, growing prolifically below the tree, but I never could find any sign of the hatchlings. My ardent hope was that, somehow, they and their mama had made it through the storm.

We never saw a Blue Jay nest in that tree again.

Another year, we placed a bird house in the same tree and were overjoyed to see a mother wren going in and out of the hole. After a few weeks, we noticed more activity, and, to our surprise, one by one, tiny fledglings emerged from the entrance. We watched as baby wrens hopped onto the perch then abruptly flew away. Within minutes, they were all gone, and that was the end of mama wren and her nest-capade.

The afternoon waned on our deck, and Mama Seagull snoozed soundly on her nest. So, we left to get some exercise and food and made our way along a beach walkway. Closer to the ocean, we could hear the waves continuously lapping along the shore. The soothing sound and the salty, fishy sea-fragrance brought back memories of family vacations.

I especially recalled one trip to Sanibel Island, Florida, in March 1986, when I was thirty-three. My son was six, and my daughter was twelve. Sweet thoughts surrounded that time with my still-young parents and children. The sun-drenched weather, dolphin-spotting boat trip around the bay, and the sound of my children oohing and ahhing over seashells made the week meaningful. I loved one scrapbook picture from that time where my mother and I stood with my small son between us, my arm around his narrow shoulders. The creamy-sanded beach, covered with seaweed and footprints, stretched out to eternity. The open sea beside us touched the edge of the horizon, and it's hard to tell where the water ends and the sky begins. An endless line of tall condos lined the beach. Overhead, the dark-blue sky contrasted with fluffy-white, drifting clouds. The sun attempted to shine through them to warm us. Gazing at the photo, I thought of all the things that transpired since it was taken, including the deaths of my son and my parents. And I wondered how my life would have been different if I'd been able to see into the future. Mike and I now looked for a restaurant we'd heard about in an ideal location near the water. Still in the resort, we found Chiringuito with tables and chairs filled with patrons under a thatched-roof, open-air building. We headed toward a sea of umbrellas that spread out on the other side of the restaurant. They hovered over an island of cushioned couches, chairs, and tables closer to the sandy beach. After being seated under one umbrella, a smiling waiter came over to greet us. I asked if they served paella, the famous Spanish dish I'd looked forward to sampling on this trip, and he suggested a blackened version.

"It's infused with squid ink," he reminded me, and I remembered having this once at a restaurant in Kansas City.

"That sounds great!" I enthused. "With some red sangria!"

Mike nodded, and I was excited to finally get my wish.

At Chiringuito

We couldn't have had a better view. Our table was separated by a wooden walkway from more umbrella-covered, cushioned seats. And a continuous procession of glamorous girls in skimpy beach outfits strutted past us. We enjoyed watching the parade as we waited for our food, breathing in the scent of grilled fish and the seaside smells of ocean life. My favorite vista was of an unpeopled plot of creamy sand lined with tall coconut-palms. The bending trees created whirligig shadows in the sand and led up to a long, thin peninsula, where a rock-edged walkway extended to a sea-lookout point. I imagined standing there, watching for sea creatures and then suddenly spotting a dolphin. Maybe he'd bound out of the water right in front of me and spray playfully while laughing like Flipper in the TV show.

Our waiter returned shortly with a small, round folding table to begin his performance. From my seat, I detected the aroma of grilled shrimp and pungent paella, both tickling my nose and making my mouth water. On the tabletop, he set a large, shallow metal pan with handles, heaped with the black cuisine. Next, he placed two large white plates beside the pan. On each one, he laid a lemon quarter and three large grilled shrimp. Using two big metal spoons, he stirred the paella carefully then deposited huge scoops of the black gold onto each plate. His final touch was to delicately place the shrimp on top of each paella mound, leaving the lemons to the side. He reminded me of an artist I'd seen with a palate of colors, who dramatically threw paint blotches onto a blank, white canvas, making the audience wonder what he was creating. When he turned the easel around, it revealed a perfectly-pictured image of Christ! But, in this case, I knew what the end result would be—a delicious, taste-stimulating Spanish dish.

I thought about how Roberto, the waiter on our first night at the resort, had brought out the mouth-salivating pan with two halves of browned and crusty fish—grilled, splayed, deboned, and ready to serve. With amazing precision, he'd meticulously served us with expertly-detailed focus, making sure he lifted every last bit of butter and surrounding juices from the platter to our plates. As tired as we were, we couldn't take our eyes off him. We were so appreciative of his efforts. Now, this server, with keen eyes focused, made sure we enjoyed every tasty tidbit of this black magic. I did.

Back in our room, I napped with a feeling of pleasure at experiencing a special paella in Spain, then I moved out to the balcony to resume my "mom patrol." She sat there, facing away from me. I was glad she was still there, because I enjoyed anticipating what she might do next and any reaction she might have to other birds flying by.

Not wanting to go out again for dinner, we ordered a bottle of Rioja, which a man graciously brought to us with a swirl of elegance. Along with the delightfully aromatic wine, he placed a bowl of crispy brown salted potato chips on the balcony table in front of us, and I drooled. We ate the savory appetizer, along with some crunchy sugar-coated almonds from Mija. Then I remembered our leftover paella. Our kind waiter had packed it up securely in a Styrofoam container, since we were left with way more than we could eat. I was thankful to have a small frig in the room to store it. In our travels, we weren't always blessed to have this convenience. When we did, it was nice, because we could save leftovers, in case we didn't want to eat out. I sighed as I opened the container and breathed in the pungent scent of our black treasure. We were set for the night.

The air was cool and pleasant at seventy-one degrees Fahrenheit, and we watched as the sun made its way down to touch the tiled rooftops, spreading its lengthening fingers to create a beautiful, layered, red, orange, and yellow backdrop. I glanced over to see Mama Seagull, still sitting peacefully resolute on her nest, surrounded by the color-saturated sky. She'd left only once since I sat down to watch her. A few warning squawks at other gulls was the only sound I'd heard from her.

Delights on the balcony

At that moment, I realized how much I love to just sit and look out at a lovely changing landscape. My room at home, where I like to read and write, has a gorgeous view of an ever-evolving, seasonally-changing lawn and garden. In the very back of my yard, a clematis-covered arbor opens onto a stone walkway lined with red, purple, and green coral bells, liriope, and a variety of hostas. A new wood-chip path leads past tiger lilies to a rustic cement birdbath and lifelike statues of the herons who frequent the lake nearby. I created a bird sanctuary at the end of the path by placing a variety of handmade wooden and thatched bird houses on top of four tall, upended logs. I can sometimes detect the whistled, two-note "fee-bee" of the Black-capped Chickadee, with the first note higher than the second. Or the three-note, descending "pee-ah-wee" call of the Eastern Wood-Peewee. One of my favorite sounds is the "cheery-cheery-cheery-cheery" of the Carolina Wrens as they flit around the yard, looking for food at the feeders. It's especially fun to watch the House Sparrows dancing and shaking the water from their wings as they jump in and out of the birdbath.

The pine trees right by my window provide a branch-needled screen that hides me from the neighbors' prying eyes. In the center of the yard, a humongous 100-foot-tall cottonwood tree extends its limbs to shelter a multitude of birds—hawks, woodpeckers, ravens, cardinals, and jays. The shade below its outstretched arms sweeps across the yard throughout the day as the sun hovers and moves in an arc. Mike has threatened many times to cut down this tremendous tree. He hates how it continuously sheds leaves, cotton-covered seeds, dead twigs, and other debris, especially after a storm. Every time the subject comes up, I vehemently object.

"How can you even *think* of doing that!" I cry out, thinking of all the wonderful wildlife it supports, and he always backs down.

Now, I luxuriated on our balcony in Spain as the setting sunrays painted every surrounding surface, and I sighed to see the changing colors, especially reflected from the red and orange tiles. It felt so peaceful at this moment, and I acknowledged that this was my very favorite day so far.

A lovely sunset scene

# Chapter Five
# ROMANTIC RONDA

It was exciting on this sunny Monday morning to be venturing into a town I'd wanted to experience ever since Rick Steves featured it in his television episode about southern Spain. I had read a great description of Ronda in *Spain Guides*:

"You're not really ready for how jaw-dropping Ronda is until you're standing there, right on the edge of the gorge, with that incredible view dropping away beneath you…with that famous stone bridge, Puente Nuevo, connecting the old and new parts of the town. It's the kind of place that makes you slow down and just stare….

"You'll feel like you've stepped into another era…. The Arab influences here are strong and give the whole place this slightly exotic twist. Then you've got the bullring—Plaza de Toros—one of the oldest in Spain. Even if bullfighting's not your thing, it's worth a wander round. It's more about the atmosphere and the sense of tradition that still lingers."

It's true. I discovered that this *is* how Ronda makes you feel.

Grabbing our boxed breakfasts, we hopped onto a bus with two older couples and an elderly man minus his wife. It was obvious. We were the old fogies. Maybe the company thought we needed special care and supervision! Especially after Mike and I missed the tour to Gibraltar!

On the two-hour drive to Ronda, our guide, in his forties, commented on the widespread use of renewable energy in his country. I asked him about the recent news of a widespread blackout that affected the Iberian Peninsula and parts of Portugal and France for about twenty-three hours in April. The outage led to disruptions in transportation, communication, and essential services. The reporters said it was caused by grid instability and the high percentage of renewable energy in Spain. I wondered how the citizens dealt with this crisis, so I asked.

"How did you manage without electricity for so long?"

Our guide let out a deep sigh like he was bored by the question.

"It was only for about a day," he humphed. "And we all have generators in case the power goes out."

*I guess they expect disruptions,* I said to myself, wondering, *How often do they have these service interruptions?* I'd heard of outages elsewhere, some lasting for days, and I reflected on how the people in my neighborhood would react if they had no electricity for a long period of time. I'd experienced blackouts in my area, but they only lasted for a few hours. During these precarious times, my neighbors and I would text back and forth to see if anyone knew anything as to when the power would restart. I could only imagine if this went on for more than a day and if we expected these occurrences on a regular basis.

The drive took us to a bus parking area in Ronda, and we ran into a café to use the restrooms and grab a cup of coffee. Standing around our bus, we sipped our caffeine infusions and breathed in the strong espresso-like aroma. Then our small group set off to see the oldest bullring in the world, according to our guide.

I didn't realize until later the significance of one building we passed on our way to Plaza de Toros. The Church of Our Lady of Mercy or

Iglesia de Nuestra Señora de la Merced was a prominent white edifice outlined with tan brick and decorated with many front-facing rectangular and round windows. Over the large, arched-stone doorway, a mysterious statue stood inside a portico. Realizing the historical significance of the building and what it represented, I pondered if it was St. John of the Cross. The sight of this statue set off many reflections on things I'd heard and read over the years.

Our Lady of Mercy in Ronda

I knew that St. John of the Cross was a Spanish Roman Catholic priest and Carmelite friar. He was known for his writings about the development of the soul. Mentored by Teresa of Avila, he became a major figure in the Counter Reformation, a period of Catholic resurgence in Spain like the Protestant Reformations of the 16th century. I learned that this building in Ronda is where he and St. Teresa initiated that reform. The site became a convent for nuns and priests of the Discalced

Carmelites—a branch of the Carmelite Order in the Catholic Church. Discalced means "without shoes" because of their commitment to poverty, simplicity, and adherence to contemplative traditions. Their focus is on prayer, community life, and austerity.

The founders of this basilica meant something special to me, because I'd read so many of the writings by St. John and St. Teresa. I admired their deep, personal relationship with Christ—something I strove to achieve. Their devotion also reminded me of St. Francis of Assisi and the Franciscan movement he initiated in the 12th century. I always admired St. Francis because of how he dramatically changed the focus of the Catholic church. He moved the emphasis away from indulgences and attaining material things to what was spiritual and eternal. His example of simplicity, with a focus on prayer, changed many peoples' lives and pushed the church's leadership in a new direction.

Thinking of St. Francis, I was reminded of a meaningful encounter I'd had in 2013. While traveling through Italy, I went to Assisi and viewed the Basilica of St. Francis there. Gazing up at Giotto's paintings of Francis's life and ministry on the walls of the upper part of the church, I was deeply moved by one picture. It portrayed Francis laying on his back in a bed while others hovered around him. He suffered from ill health during much of his life but still ministered to many people. The painting struck me because, at the time, my son lay suppine in a bed, suffering from lung cancer, a disease he'd endured for over twelve years. Yet Phil, like Francis, still ministered and witnessed his faith to those around him. Even as he struggled to breathe in the hospital, after one surgery, he shared his hope and faith in an eternal God, who cared for him and would one day welcome him home. I loved that about my son.

Gazing at the basilica now, and guessing about the mysterious statue, I thought about the Carmelites and Catholics in general. Their beliefs were passionate and inspirational, but they differed from the Protestant churches I'd attended. Both approaches follow Jesus Christ, but they part ways in their approaches—their views on authority, ways to salvation, practice of the sacraments, structure, etc. When I trekked along the Camino de Santiago, I was awed by the local cathedrals and dumbfounded by the Cathedral of Santiago de Compostela. The worshippers in these gilded sanctuaries captured my heart when I saw their love for Jesus—a passion I share. I'm learning that each of us come to God in our own special way. While traversing our paths, He speaks to us individually through the spirit that works inside us when we believe in His Son. I appreciate my own special callings, and I want to be able to use the particular gifts He's given me to help others. Some may be led to follow in a different way. It's up to God how He directs and leads us as we turn to Him.

Moving on from the church, we entered Alameda del Tajo Park, a historic park that offered stunning views of a canyon and surrounding valleys along shady pathways. Still heading toward the bullring, I noticed several plaques in the park to honor people like Orson Welles and Ernest Hemingway. Glancing away from these reminders of Ronda's famous visitors, something entirely different grabbed my attention. A life-size, bronze statue of a woman stood proudly in an elaborate costume. I stopped to gaze at her, intrigued by her beauty and what she might represent. Lips pursed in a dignified expression, her long curls were pulled back under an ornate tiara. She wore a low-cut, richly-detailed gown with huge, puffed sleeves covered in tiny round decorations. The bodice of her dress was patterned with swirling designs, and around her neck, a circular pendant symbolized something only she might understand. She held a fan carved with ornate motifs, and a small, embroidered bag hung from her wrist. Her posture was poised and noble, with one hand resting at her hip. I discovered that she was inspired by Francisco Goya. Named Lady Goyesca, she paid tribute to the 18th century ladies of the annual Ronda fair.

Now, closer to the ring, prominent figures of masculine matadors lined the walkways and captured my attention.

El Niño de la Palma

A replica of Cayetano Ordóñez, known as El Niño de la Palma, or "The Boy from La Palma," posed near the bullring entrance. Flinging his cape dramatically behind him, he was the patriarch of the Ordóñez family of bullfighters. He was also the matador who inspired the character of Pedro Romero in Hemingway's book, *The Sun Also Rises*. A bronze statue of his son, Antonio, stood solemnly nearby, his cape held down solemnly at his side.

Approaching the bullring, a huge brownstone, emblem-decorated gate hovered officiously as if warily deciding who could enter its arched metal entryway. White-washed walls extended from either side of the gate to surround the ring. Nearby, a large bronze bull snorted and stamped his feet inside a circular, iron-fenced enclosure. I was enthralled by his ferocity. His huge horns protruded threateningly to create the illusion of impending danger.

The bull by Plaza de Toros

Inside the bowels of the bullring, a narrow corridor led us past the bullfighters' chapel. I wondered how many matadors, filled with trepidation before entering the ring and facing the angry bulls, stepped inside this sanctuary, hoping to allay their fears. We peeked inside claustrophobically small, white-washed rooms that hold the large bulls tightly, and almost inhumanely, enclosed. Heavy wooden doors and sealed windows prevented their escape. The bulls were allowed no exposure to humans before their dramatic exits into the ring. I sensed the terror they might feel as I looked around the suffocating room. My heart pounded as I pictured a frightened, frustrated beast feeling trapped and wondering what he might face next. Snorting, he breathed in the dust as he stamped his hooves on the dirt floor, and it filled his lungs. I could taste the metallic graininess of the tiny particles in the back of my own throat. I imagined him butting his horns against a wall. He was desperate to be free. I started to sweat, feeling myself trapped. I quickly walked out of the suffocating enclosure.

A stone-arched entry ushered us out of the dark corridor into the ring, and the sunlight that glared into the opening was almost blinding. I walked through it and felt relieved as I stood looking around the large, circular ring. I thought about how the bull must feel when he entered this space. Did he feel relieved after being confined? Or did he grow more frightened when men swinging capes rushed toward him with piercing instruments?

Shuffling through the caramel-colored sand that covered the arena floor and puffed up like smoke around our feet as we walked, we breathed in more dust. We gazed around the 360-degree enclosure at the tiered seats that stair-stepped up from the stadium. The honored seats were directly above the arched entry where the bulls entered the ring. Only the elites were allowed to sit there.

Elaborate matador outfits

Outside the arena, we stepped through halls lined with the pictorial history of bullfighting. Glass cases filled with colorful matador mementos surrounded us. I was especially impressed by a bright pink capa de brega or capote—a bullfighter's cape. It matched the matador's costume—pink leggings and tight-fitting, embroidered knickers and jacket.

I wondered if the bulls were irritated by the colorful muleta, or small cape waved by the matador. As it turned out, they are color-blind, and what bothers them most is the movement of the cape.

One painting colorfully portrayed the lurid details of an ancient bullfight in a medieval Spanish town, where the matador was struck down by the bull. It was a gory scene. Not one I would want to witness in person. But I could imagine myself standing to the side, along with other citizens, watching this fight unfold in the square. Detecting the iron-scent of shed blood, I might feel shocked as someone I knew was horribly gored. I would feel my sympathies lessening for the huge animal as I watched my friends trying to pull the man away without getting impaled by the raging beast.

Turning from the picture, I wanted to know more about these matadors and their passion for this blood-sport. I discovered that Francisco Romero, grandfather of Pedro Romero, "is generally regarded as having been the first to introduce the practice of fighting bulls on foot around 1726...." said *Wikipedia*. "This type of fighting drew more attention from the crowds. Thus the modern corrida, or fight, began to take form, as riding noblemen were replaced by commoners on foot. This new style prompted the construction of dedicated bullrings, initially square, and later round, to discourage the cornering of the action."

Looking up, I was mesmerized by another painting with Pedro Romero proudly donning a decorated red jacket and a lacy white jabot. His dark eyes, graceful nose, and thin, sensitive lips were prominently bound by bushy sideburns that swept down to his chin to make him look more masculine. The picture aptly captured someone who appeared vulnerable but wanted his audience to know he was a man's man. I was very curious what his life was like, especially his family situation. This was a man who constantly faced dramatic, life-altering peril in the ring. How did his relatives feel about this? Did other family members participate in this dangerous sport?

Painting of Pedro Romero

Here's what I discovered. Born in Ronda, Pedro Romero lived from 1754 to 1839 and learned the art of bullfighting from his grandfather, Francisco, and his father, Juan. As a youth, he participated in bullfights with Juan in Algeciras, Seville, and Madrid, Spain. In 1776, at age twenty-two, his reputation exploded when he killed 285 bulls. Before retiring in 1799, he had killed a total of 5,558 bulls. He was the first matador to present bullfighting as an artform and a display of courage. After retiring, he became head of a bullfighting school in Seville, where he influenced many with his knowledge of the skill.

His father had a total of six sons. Four of them became bullfighters: Gaspar, Antonio, José, and Pedro. Sadly, Gaspar died in a bullfight in 1773, while serving as a banderillero, or assistant, to his father. Antonio was also killed by a bull in Granada in 1802. Thinking how traumatic my own son's death was to me, I wondered how Father Juan and his wife must have felt about these tragedies. The mother must have worried every time her husband and sons stepped into a ring. My heart ached just thinking about it.

Of all the brothers, Pedro is best-known in bullfighting history. He never married or had children, and I wondered if he didn't want to subject his own sons to this life of constant insecurity and fear. Again, I cringed to think of having children subjected to such imminent brutality.

After making our way through the museum, we couldn't avoid the gift shop, on the way out, and I fell in love with a gorgeous, wide-brimmed, turquoise straw hat. I bought it and placed it on my head. *Just what I needed!* I thought as I stepped outside into the bright sunlight, wearing it proudly. It made me feel like someone famous—a Spanish movie star hiding my fame under a big hat and sunglasses. On the practical side, it matched my outfit and provided my face with needed shade as we trekked through the now-heated streets toward Puente Nuevo, or "New Bridge."

My attention refocused as we approached the largest of three bridges spanning the 390-foot chasm that carries the Guadelevin River and divides the city of Ronda. I was impressed by this amazing structure that took thirty-four years to build, starting in 1759. Scenes between the iron bars along the bridge were spectacular. Looking down, I was captivated by a terraced café with umbrella-covered tables overlooking the yawning, humongous mouth of a gorge. From a landing beyond the bridge, I gazed down at the ravine, breathing in the earthy smell of the rocks along the sides and feeling the refreshing moistness of churning water that rippled far below. I took in as much as I could, feeling overwhelmed by the huge, creviced limestone crags that forced their way up hundreds of feet from the stream. Capped by greenery on all sides, the bulging bluffs displayed prominent multi-storied buildings with terraces that offered breathtaking views of the valley below. This site alone made it worth spending a day in Ronda.

But I wondered how Mike felt as I stood gazing down, since he suffered from vertigo. He didn't hide his feelings when I teasingly motioned for him to come closer to the edge, so I could show him the stunning scene. He cautiously crept closer, staying at least a few feet from where I leaned over the iron fencing that separated me from the steep cliffs and burbling creek below.

From the rock-topped promontory, our guide pointed out a chamber built into the impressive arched bridge. It was once used as a prison and torture chamber for POWs during the Spanish Civil War, between 1936 and 1939. Especially dangerous prisoners were thrown from the windows of the chamber to the bottom of the gorge. I could envision the bodies being catapulted down, screaming as they fell to the bottom into the rushing stream. *Yikes!* The chamber is now used as an exhibition for the bridge's history. *Thank God!*

A scene of the gorge in Ronda

We approached midday, and I had to press my way between the multiplying tourists as we tried to escape from the bridge. Finally free from the crowds, some from our group wondered how the townspeople felt about the growing presence of pushy visitors. On our walk back to the bus, our guide shared his thoughts on the topic.

"It depends on what you mean by 'tourist,'" he answered cryptically, and we all stepped closer to hear what he would say. "We welcome people like you, who are respectful of our ways, want to learn about our customs and history, and are willing to spend money to help our economy. But we dislike those who tramp through our streets as sightseers, stay in the cheapest places, treat our people like servants, and spend nothing to support the local economy. They rent spaces in our buildings and drive up the prices, so the locals must pay more for a house. Of course, the Spanish people don't like this."

No one said a word in response. We all just hoped that he approved of *us* being here. Well, we had paid him to be our guide! I thought he *might* appreciate our business! But I wondered if he alluded to the people who frequented the Camino de Santiago on trails that led through Spain to Santiago de Compostela. They carried backpacks and stayed in albergues, like hostels, and spent little money in the towns they traveled through. I hoped the Spanish people were not getting tired of these pilgrims, because the experience I had while trekking over the Camino was so life changing, and I knew it was for others who made the journey.

Next up was LA Almazara—a thematic museum and organic olive oil farm. Conceived by designer Philippe Starck, "...it is a museum and cultural center that pays homage to Andalusian tradition and the art of olive oil production," according to their website. Apparently, in 2010, two Andalusian entrepreneurs toured some Spanish wineries and noticed how architects, like Frank Gehry, had transformed wine tourism. They envisioned something similar in Andalusia using olive oil. Unsuccessful at first, they realized they needed to rename the vineyard, giving it a more Spanish name, thus the birth of LA Almazara.

Entering a huge reddish-brown square building, my eyes were drawn to a horn jutting out of one side and an oval-shaped form on another side. We were told that they exemplified cubism and symbolized the horns and testicles of a bull. *Hmmm,* I said to myself. *Pretty creative!* Besides having a vivid imagination, the architect gravitated toward darkness, because it was *very* dark inside. I wondered if they were trying to save on electricity. I had to feel my way around the museum until my eyes adjusted. The only visible color came from something mystical on the ceiling. A huge painting hovered over us—a swirl of bulls, olives, and wings created by the architect's daughter. It loomed mysteriously, and we were told it symbolized the peasants. *If you say so.*

The main building at LA Almazara

We moved through more dark halls, breathing in the earthy, clayish interior smell and following the sound of our guide's voice. I watched my footing, especially as we felt our way precariously down obscure, unlit steps. In another large room, the guide pointed out narrow passageways with walls covered by lengthy, tiny-lettered texts that gave the history of olives in the region. I wondered how the seniors in our group would manage this part of the tour, especially with our squinty eyes and dog-tired legs after standing, walking, and sightseeing all morning. I harumphed.

"Spain produces forty-five percent of the world's olive oil," the guide began, trying to build our interest. But, at that moment, I boldly approached another guide with a desperate plea. "Where can I find a restroom?" Mike, beside me, nodded in agreement, and the man motioned for us to follow him, as the rest of the group made their way down the narrow halls to experience the "fascinating" olive oil history. Up an elevator to another floor then down a dimly-lit hall, we finally found the facilities, almost hidden from view. With no other human in sight, I made my way in and out and hoped the guide was waiting to show me the way back to the group. The echoing walls felt eerily empty, and I knew I could easily get lost. Plus, I wondered what exactly was behind the walls. *Were they hiding something they didn't want the tourists to see?* I could feel the hair rising on the back of my neck.

Suddenly, Mike exited the men's room, and we both spotted the guide waiting down the hall. Taking the elevator to the large room where we'd left the group, we realized, *Oh darn it! We missed the oil-history tour.* We were just in time for an excursion to the vineyards! Yay! Greeted by sparkling sunlight, I breathed in fresh air as we made our way to a dirt road. We passed by one last creepy artifact—an amorphic, unnamed human replica with water pouring over its head. Symbolic of what—I didn't know. Nor did I care.

Up a hill, we stood on a platform overlooking a valley with views of olive trees. After more ad nauseum history of the importance of olive oil, we made our way toward a greenhouse for an oil tasting and lunch. Brown bottles of olive oil sat waiting on long benched tables under a patio awning at the entrance to a building. Mike and I found two seats together as a man stood to one side and instructed us on the right way to taste oil. Holding up one bottle after another, he poured a little of the liquid into a ceramic spoon then sipped and swished it around his mouth, breathing in before swallowing. He had us do the same thing to identify flavors like grassy, fruity, buttery, peppery, or spicy. That way, we compared what was in each bottle. He explained why extra virgin olive oil is of the highest quality, being extracted through a pressing of fresh olives without heat or chemicals. With a low acidity level and superior flavor, "it's free from defects like rancidity or mustiness," he said. "It's also healthier, since the process preserves the oil's natural antioxidants, vitamins, and minerals.

"When you buy olive oil, make sure it is 100 percent made in Spain," he emphasized. "It shouldn't come from a mix of origins. That would dilute the quality."

*Very interesting,* I thought, considering the huge bottles of olive oil we saw in Costco. Now I wondered where it came from. My guess was multiple regions.

After a while, the people at our table began to grow a bit cantankerous, mumbling under their oil-saturated breath. They were understandably impatient, especially since the tasting lingered far longer than we'd anticipated. We were hot, tour-tired, exhausted, and our stomachs were growling.

*"To heck with the oil!"* one person huffed, loud enough for everyone to hear. *"Bring us some wine!"*

It felt like a riot brewing, and I wondered if the people at my table were going to start banging their knives and forks on the table and chanting. It made me a little nervous, and I imagined our hosts whispering, "How ill-mannered! Those terrible Americans! They're all the same!"

I breathed a sigh of relief when the oil-tasting tirade finally came to an end. But I was shocked by the sudden whirlwind of activity as the people at our table dove into baskets of bread placed quickly in front of them. It was like we were all half-starved refugees. Slices in hand, we dipped the bread into saucers filled with oil and local vinegar. I poured the most peppery versions onto my small plate then savored each spicy taste on my tongue. *Yum!* But the best was yet to come. A large serving plate of Iberian ham slices and payoyo cheese arrived, and everyone dove in hungrily with their forks. The melt-in-your-mouth ham and cheese made us all sigh with delight.

Known as jamón ibérico de bellota, the ham comes from Iberian pigs, native to Spain and Portugal. It's known for its rich, nutty flavor, since the pigs are raised on acorns. A strong cheese that tastes spicy and slightly salty, payoyo comes from the milk of Spanish payoya goats and merina sheep.

Dishes of sauteed vegetables, salads full of tomatoes and cucumbers, tomato paté, tortillas or Spanish omelettes, and pie came in a succession, with plenty of Rioja wine. Everyone at our table mmmed with delight, since we were more than ready for some tasty food and glasses of refreshing wine. This meal was clearly the highlight of our cubist olive oil factory tour.

That night, at the Sea Grill, Mike and I breathed in the salty ocean air as we gazed out at tall palm trees and unusual grass-topped umbrellas, where people sipped sangrias. Staring out at the water, we watched strollers leisurely make their way down a sandy sidewalk. Gazpacho was my first course, and I savored every creamy, spicy, tomatoey taste. My tongue didn't quite know what to do with this cold soup but decided it was quite acceptable. I ate it very slowly, before my huge prawn arrived. Although the shrimp was delicious, I had to fight for every bite. The tightly-gripping shell did *not* want to give up its rich contents. Not being familiar with how to eat it properly, I struggled to dig out the meat with a small fork. It took quite some time, but I appreciated it more because it was so hard to retrieve. Mike made a wiser choice and ordered the grilled turbot, which looked especially appealing as I struggled with my resistant dish. I smelled the fragrance of his buttery grilled fish from where I sat as I fought my prawn. He rolled his eyes and licked his lips teasingly as he brought each bite up to his mouth.

The dessert was the best surprise of the night. It was a sweet coconut sorbet topped with small cubes of tart pineapple, crumbles of nutty, toasted almond and tangy dark chocolate, and fresh-chopped mint. A slice of lime sat on the side. Unbelievable! Each bite literally melted in my mouth as I tasted the coconutty, tart, fruity combination of flavors.

Our view from the Sea Grill

We faced the beach, enjoying the last bites of dessert at our table, along with breezes and surf smells that wafted toward us. Then I happened to turn around, and I noticed an adorable small white dog under the table behind us. *He looks just like Barney!* I thought, and my heart skipped a beat. I felt sad, missing my furry friend and wondering how he was doing back home. Meal finished, I decided to meet this little guy.

"I saw your dog!" I boldly walked over to the nice-looking couple. They appeared way more sophisticated than us, but I'd learned not to let appearances keep me from talking to people. "He looks just like ours!" I pulled out my phone to show them a picture of Barney.

"Yes! He does!" The wife beamed between bites of a salad, gazing at my photo. "What kind of dog is he?"

"A shweenie—half dachshund, half shi tzu." I smiled, thinking how few people had ever heard of this funny mix. Most people nodded with a vacant look on their face when I tried to explain.

"Baxter is part shi tzu and part schnauzer." She nodded with familiarity.

"Oh! That's interesting," I said, relieved that at least she could relate to our odd mix.

"Where are you from?" she prompted.

"From near Kansas City, Missouri," I responded, "and you?"

"We're from London," the husband offered.

Peter and Mary had other homes, including one in Costa del Sol. They traveled a lot because of his work, which had something to do with international tax. I wondered if he was a lawyer or an accountant but didn't ask. His business took them all over the world, they explained, and wherever they went, Baxter tagged along.

"We would like to take our dogs with us, but we don't think they'd do very well on planes, especially our corgi." I sighed, thinking how nice it would be to have them with us while we travel, at least part of the time.

"Oh, we use K9 Jets," she explained. "They're a private jet service that allows you to travel with your pets uncaged. They fly all over!"

"I've never heard of them," I said curiously. "I'll check them out."

I found out later that the service is limited. It only flies to certain places in Europe, the Middle East, and the United States. I thought it was a great idea, if you happened to be going to one of their destinations.

"We were in England one year ago," I changed the subject. "We did a walking tour through the Cotswolds and loved it!"

"Oh!" Mary's face lit up. "What towns did you visit?"

"The first one was Moreton-in-Marsh," I recalled.

"We have a cottage there!" she exclaimed unexpectedly.

"What a coincidence!" I said, leaning closer. "That's where our walk started and ended. We loved it."

"Where did you stay?" she wondered, gazing up at me.

"The White Hart Royal Inn." I smiled. "We loved the place and the trip so much that I wrote a book about it. It will be released in the next couple of months."

"Oh, what is it called?"

*"Lessons from the Cotswolds."*

Mary typed in the name on her phone and AI pulled up quite a bit of information about the book and me. I was stunned!

"Please text me when it's out!" She was excited. So was I. "I want to get the book!"

I put her name and number into my phone, and I promised to let them know. It seemed so coincidental that they had a house in the town we'd frequented twice on our journey. Small world! But, really, I don't believe in coincidences anymore. To me, it was just another God wink!

That was the perfect ending to a day packed with many unique experiences—new places, captivating scenery, breathtaking views, unusual tours, wonderful wine, palatable olive oil, and flavorful food. What more could we ask? All I could hope for was even more of the same the next day. Well, we would have to wait and see!

# MARVELOUS MáLaga

This was the last time and Mike knew it! It was his final chance to appreciate the amazing, varied breakfast at the Sea Grill. So, he savored every mouthful from multiple plates filled with colorful, flavorful dainties, while I took nips of my berry-loaded yoghurt, along with chia pudding and tongue-biting sips of ginger juice. Then we headed to meet a group bound for Málaga.

The second-most populous city in Andalusia, Málaga has about 590,000 people. Founded around 770 BC by the Phoenicians, it's one of the oldest continuously inhabited cities in Western Europe. Once known as Malaca, it's been under the thumb of Carthage, Rome, the Visigoths, the Byzantine Empire, Arab and Berber forces, and

Mike's last breakfast at the Sea Grill

the Crown of Castile. Now known mainly for tourism and technology, it's the home of Pablo Picasso and Antonio Banderos. The port has played an important role as a stopover for international and regional trade on routes between the Mediterranean and Atlantic Seas.

During our hour-long drive, I was surprised when our guide, David, from the tour to Gibraltar, brought up the subject of Spanish healthcare and explained the pros and cons. Known as the National Health System (SNS), it provides free or low-cost access to healthcare for all legal residents through social security contributions, he said. Payment rates run about six and a half percent of pay by employees to thirty percent by employers, with variations based on salaries and needs. Citizens are responsible for up to sixty percent of the cost of health products like prescriptions, orthotics, and prosthetics. Though many liked the "free" services, they discovered some inherent problems. The wait times for the public healthcare services were often so long that many opted for private insurance to supplement the public coverage. Another unexpected problem was visitations. David explained that many people hung out at the facilities, coming daily to take advantage of the services. Since they could not be refused care, they often misused the system. I thought this was interesting, and I wondered again about the costs and benefits of universal healthcare.

Our first stop in Málaga was a café, Casa Aranda, where we crunched on sweet churros dipped in thick hot chocolate. Like long, crispy-fried doughnuts, they were so intensely rich I could only eat part of one! The nose-tingling sweet milk-chocolate smell was enough for me.

Next stop, the gorgeous Cathedral of Málaga, known formally as Incarnation Cathedral or Catedral de la Encarnación. Also called "La Manquita," or "The One-Armed Lady," one of its towers was never completed because of financial difficulties. Founded in the 16th century, this Roman Catholic church was built on the site where the city's main mosque stood during eight centuries of Muslim rule.

"La Manquita"

Inside the massive cathedral doors, we were greeted with the scent of ancient wood—a blend of musty, earthy smells with hints of leather. Impressive wooden choir stalls stood out prominently in the central nave. The figures of forty-two apostles, Mary, and some bishops were meticulously carved into the stalls, which were classified as the eighth wonder of the world in the 18th century! In the middle of the floor, where tourists stood staring at the stall carvings, I noticed a huge, three-sided wooden structure. A small cupola holding Mary and a cross sat on top of a four-sided roof that looked like a hat. I wondered if it was an incense burner, but I couldn't find a description of it in my brochure or on the internet. *Who knows what it is?* I puzzled.

The mysterious centerpiece

I found the inside of the cathedral to feel more like a museum than a place of worship. But then something caught my eye and inspired a deeper understanding of what might lie hidden beneath the layered antiquity of the place. I was drawn to a painting on a wall above the stalls. It was a large, oval portrait of a man in a dark cloak raising one hand up to heaven. Below colorful stained-glass windows and above an altar, it captured my imagination. I discovered it portrayed St. Francis Caracciolo (1563-1608), who was an Italian Roman Catholic priest and co-founder of the Congregation of the Clerics Regular Minor or Caracciolini. This saint was known for his devotion and his practice of spending extended periods of time in adoration. That was the reason for the hand raised in praise. It reminded me of prayer nights at our church, when many gather to sing and worship. During songs, people boldly lift their hands in praise to God. This practice actually has a name. It's called "orans," a Latin word meaning one who is praying, or "orant," lifting up holy hands (from 1 Timothy 2:8).

Still looking up, my attention was captured by another highlight in the cathedral. Two huge pipe organs stood prominently above the choir stalls. Rare examples of 18th century instruments in good working condition, they can emit an astonishing sound. Baroque-styled with Rococo ornamentation, Corinthian columns, and gilded figures, each one was over seventy-two feet tall with three fifty-one-note keyboards and over 4,000 pipes. Considered a significant part of Spain's musical heritage, they represented an outstanding artistic and technical achievement of the Baroque era.

The cathedral's southern entrance was called Puerta del Sol, or "Sun's Door." Twin towers rose on either side of the enormous arched entryway, where a huge double-sided door stood, covered with impressive carvings. Depictions of Mary's annunciation, the moment when the angel announced to Mary that she would bear the Christ child, were meant to capture the viewer's attention. But my eyes grew wide, and I took a deep breath when I realized what was pictured at the very top of each double door—scallop shells. In Spain, these shells symbolized the Camino de Santiago and the spiritual journey of Christians as "pilgrims and strangers on the earth." The shells were also a sign for rebirth. But I was especially amazed that, even here in a southern Spanish town, I was reminded of the Camino and my own pilgrimage to Santiago de Compostela.

I discovered another fascinating carved image on the door, below the scene of Mary. A sailboat stood mysteriously, and I wondered what it meant. I realized that boats represented the Church and the community of believers navigating the seas of life and finding safety and guidance in Christ. The nave of the church underscored this significance.

The magnificent cathedral door

A boat also stood for the believer's voyage of faith. Like Noah's ark, it represented protection and salvation amidst the storms of life. Think of Jesus in the boat with the disciples during a tempest. Connected to the annunciation, it referred to the beginning of Mary's journey as one through whom salvation entered the world. A coastal city, Málaga also has a strong maritime heritage. Fishing boats, called jabegas, often symbolized the town. Now I understood that the boat carving served as a reminder of many things: the Christian faith, the Church's role in guiding believers, and as a nod to the city's relationship with the sea. All in the context of an annunciation scene! *Amazing!*

Too much information? Well, now we were off to see another town highlight. The Alcazaba is one of the best-preserved Muslim fortified palaces. Dating back to the Middle Ages, I can only tell you what we did *not* see! My interest piqued at first, as I wondered, *What is an alcazaba?* The term came from the Arabic, al-qasaba, meaning "the citadel" or "urban fortress." I thought about the word, casbah, and wondered if it came from the same word. Well, it does! This type of fortified building or complex could be found in Spain and North Africa, usually in the heart of a Muslim city. It housed residents and rulers in a walled-off section designed for defense. Featuring strong walls, towers, and gates, it was built on a hill for maximum advantage.

Standing at the bottom of the fortress, I took one look at all the steps that led up to The Alcazaba. I glanced over at Mike, who was shaking his head. It was a non-starter. While our group geared up for the uphill climb, we stood mesmerized by a gold-sprayed mime standing on one leg. Wearing a headband, with his mouth open, he held a tennis racket and stood precariously on a cement block with a sign that read, "Artista de Africa." I'm sure he was supposed to be a famous Spanish tennis-player. The younger crowd looking on related more to the mime than us old fogies, who weren't so taken with current sports figures or idols.

The mime near The Alcazaba

On our way to The Alcazaba, I'd noticed many appealing shops and cafés. I thought, *It sure would be nice to sit and sip a cool drink about now!*

Fanning ourselves from the rising heat, I knew Mike would appreciate a few moments to rest. What's nice about being older is we always had a good excuse for not overly exerting ourselves. I could just say, "I'm so sorry but, you know, we just need to pass on that" while slyly pointing with a wink and a nod to Mike. No one ever objected or asked why. We got out of so many things we don't want to do!

Well, as we stood looking at the steep climb and feeling the heat, our guide mercifully gave us an out. We could go with him all the way to the top, he said, or we could stay behind and meet the group at this location in an hour and a half. Mike and I looked at each other. We didn't need to think about it. We turned to find a nearby café. As we walked away, we spotted another older couple we'd met on the bus. They were going in the same direction.

"Can we join you?" I asked boldly.

Leslie and Jud smiled and nodded pleasantly. We all headed to the nearest sidewalk café, found a shaded table, and ordered drinks. Leslie and I finished our drinks quickly with the same idea.

"I want to check out the shops," she announced.

*"So do I!"* I beamed.

Leslie and I jumped up and left the men enjoying their beers in the shade, happy to not have to go with us. Fortunately, we had similar taste in what we were looking for. We found a shop down the street with shelves and walls full of colorful, hand-painted, locally-made creations. She found a perfect Spanish souvenir—a Picasso-designed bull. I left, not sadly, without a thing. Over the years on our trips, I've collected ceramic tiles, refrigerator magnets, shot glasses, paintings, and other paraphernalia. After accumulating boxes of these things and running out of wall, refrigerator, and cupboard space, I ended up giving many of them away. Now, what I sometimes looked for are tiny bowls for the vitamins and pills I take. But, for some reason, these are not easy to find. *Well, it wasn't as though I really needed them!* I thought. Anyway, it was fun to browse through the shop at all the colorful, handmade items. Some were very creative, like colorful ceramic bulls and Spanish people dressed in different costumes. Too bad I had no space for them at home. *That's what happens when you get older,* I chuckled to myself. *Good or bad, you run out of room. I guess it's mostly good, since you save so much money on things you used to buy!*

We stood in the courtyard at the bottom of the steps to The Alcazaba. I watched as the remainder of our group descended, looking bedraggled and wilted in the heat, especially the older couples. *Thank God we didn't go!* I thought, wondering if the site was worth all that sweaty effort. I'd never know. I'm sure it was memorable, even if it was in an "I'll never do that again" way! *Ha, ha!* I felt like our time was well-spent. We'd enjoyed getting to know another couple—sharing a cold drink and experiencing a special shopping adventure. All good!

No one talked on the hour-long bus ride back to Puente Romano. I didn't blame them. We were all hot and exhausted. It'd been a long day, and we anticipated the last-night banquet. I knew it would be special. They always were on these company trips. The meal would be over the top, and you just never knew what amazing entertainment they'd provide.

What I didn't look forward to was getting up at 2:15 in the morning for a bag pull at 2:50 and a 3:15 ride to the airport so we'd be early enough to check in for a 5:55 flight to Paris. There was no telling how that would go! God only knew. *Arg!*

<h1 style="text-align:center">Chapter Seven<br>FABULOUS FLAMENCO</h1>

It was our last night in Costa del Sol, and I wondered what God had up His sleeve. The week had gone well. I had no complaints. Our room with its amazing balcony view was beyond what I could have dreamt for. The day trips and food, especially my bucket-list item, paella, were exceptional. And even the one catastrophe of missing the Gibraltar tour had ended well with an unexpectedly pleasant sailboat ride. But there was one very important thing missing, and I hated to leave Andalusia without experiencing it. *Flamenco!*

If you've never watched flamenco dancing, you might not understand why it was so important for me to see it again. A very expressive Spanish art form that combines singing, guitar-playing, and dancing, it is characterized by its emotional intensity, intricate footwork, and hand movements. I'd only seen it once, in Scottsdale, Arizona, at a Spanish restaurant twenty years ago. Ever since then, I'd wanted to feel again the heart-throbbing, rhythmic feet-stomping, shawl-swinging, hip-thrusting action. Of course, it must be backed by the sensational strumming of an expert guitarist or two. I can't explain it. I just know that, like the famous fado singers in Portugal, the passion of flamenco dancing is something you just have to experience for yourself, at least once in your lifetime. Since I'd only watched it once, and I hoped to feel its energy and breathe in its exuberance at least once more. I thought, *What better place to encounter it than here in its place of origin—Andalusia.* Sadly, it hadn't happened, and disappointment welled up inside me.

I'd missed it once while here. The first night, when we were sitting outside in the courtyard, served by Roberto while eating the wonderful fish and drinking the amazing local wine, I'd caught a glimpse of a dancer inside the restaurant. I'd also seen a group of girls decked out in beautiful long dresses going inside to join a party, and I'd wrongly assumed it was a private event. So, I sat outside, wondering what I might be missing and wishing that I could see the performance inside, since the Spanish music I heard was completely captivating. Later, I found out El Pimpi Restaurant had dancers performing flamenco every night after 9 pm! Being seniors who like to hit the sack early so we can rise at the crack of dawn, it was the one and only night we stayed up that late. *Shoot!*

Now, I wondered if we'd leave without *once* being emotionally pulled into the tap, pound, tap, lunge, tap, swoop, tap, swing of a flamboyant flamenco dancer.

This feeling of disappointment reminded me of our trip to Rio de Janeiro in 2004. I remember being so excited to experience the sights, and especially the sounds, of this mesmerizingly picturesque place. I romanticized the scenes from movies, like the 1979 James Bond film, *Moonraker,* that included many mysterious and captivating views of the city. During our stay, my dream was to experience the famous Brazilian dancing and music—samba and bossa nova. Samba was a lively Brazilian-style music, rooted in African traditions and known for its characteristic rhythms, percussion instruments, and Portuguese lyrics. Bossa nova was a Brazilian musical genre that emerged in the late 1950s. Blending samba with jazz, it was characterized by a relaxed, syncopated rhythm, sophisticated harmony, and melancholic melodies. The term bossa nova meant "new trend" or "new wave" in Portuguese.

We rendezvoused with relatives who lived in Brazil on that trip, and, sadly, they had something else in mind for our last night in Rio. Though I told them how much I wanted to experience the local music, they thought this was way too touristy. So, they drove us through side streets and down dark alleys until we arrived at a place they'd wanted to go and talked excitedly about. My curiosity piqued, and I wondered what this amazing venue could be. Well…. We pulled up in front of what looked like a dive bar. When we went in, my suspicions were confirmed. It *was* a dive bar! We entered a smoke-filled, dimly-lit room and sat at an ancient wood table. The walls were old and shabby, obviously never painted or updated since it opened, maybe sometime in the last century? The place reminded me of a London tavern dating back to the 1800s. From what I recalled, we were the only ones in the place! I've happily forgotten the name of the venue. As it turned out, the obscurity of the bar was exactly why they'd selected it. Apparently, their church didn't approve of drinking, and they wanted to go to a little-known place so they could imbibe without being recognized. I spent that uneventful evening trying to appreciate the cultural ambiance of this doleful, forgettable place. When we left Rio the next morning, I perused the airport shops to find CDs of famous bossa nova singers from the area. I was so disappointed I'd missed hearing any live music while we were there.

Now, on my last night in Spain, I didn't want to experience this same awful regret of never seeing any flamenco while in Andalusia. I sighed as we dressed up to go down and join our group for the final banquet. In our fancy shoes, we stepped cautiously down the tiled steps from our room and rounded the corner into the courtyard below our balcony. We immediately spotted something very unusual. Right in front of us stood a three-inch-high baby seagull on a step to the walkway. The tiny bird, covered with black-spotted, downy feathers, hopped one step at a time toward us. We stopped in our tracks, glued to the sidewalk, and watched as it descended then quickly waddled toward an alley. We followed until it disappeared down a cobbled walkway. A staff member scurried up, and we pointed after the bird. He'd seen it too, he nodded. I'm sure the people at the resort see them quite often. I tried to get pictures of the baby gull before it scooted away, but it was far too fast for me! I wondered if it was one of Mama Seagull's hatchlings. I may never know. I also wondered if this was a bright sign of things to come!

We approached our group, huddled around high-top tables in the courtyard, and one middle-aged man walked up to introduce himself. The first words out of our mouths were to tell him about the surprising sight. He shook his head. He hadn't seen the baby gull. But he told us he was from Texas and had started with our firm in 1992. *He will be the one to do the tribute at our banquet,* I thought. At the end of every company-sponsored trip, the most veteran financial advisor always made a memorable speech. It was a tribute to the son of the founder, whose remarkable vision had established and grown our firm into what it was today.

I will always remember what my husband said next. Usually in conversations, he listened quietly, but, in this case, he saw something unique in this man, and he spoke up when the financial advisor expressed concern about his speech that night.

"I can tell that you are caring and sensitive, and that you have a compassionate heart. You'll do a great job!" Mike spoke out of the blue.

After he said the words, I watched the man's face suddenly change. Tears filled his eyes, and he thanked Mike for saying this. It obviously touched him in a profound and unexpected way. I pondered his reaction. Maybe he wondered, as I did, if his many years of trying to help his clients had really paid off. Was the time spent worth all the incredible effort? Did they appreciate what he'd done for them? I'd often considered these same things. My contacts with people had frequently been met with little or no response. It was rare to hear a "Thank you."

This reminded me of when Jesus healed the ten lepers. What an amazing feat! Especially then, when anyone with this dreaded disease was completely ostracized from family and community. They had to live the rest of their lives outside the city gates in isolation to prevent contact and contamination. The Bible record in Luke 17 talked about ten of them who were set free of this devastating diagnosis. Yet only one of the lepers returned to thank Jesus! This has been my own experience. Rarely do people acknowledge service rendered or gifts offered. I was always extremely grateful for anyone who took the time to show appreciation. I imagined this man felt the same way. Here was someone he had just met, telling him in his own way that his life had been worth living, that people did appreciate all the years he'd spent helping them. I was so proud of Mike and this insight offered. What a gift to this man we'd just met!

Inside the banquet room, next to the courtyard, we found a white-clothed table close to the front and to the left of a stage. This ended up being a perfect location for experiencing the evening activities. Looking down at the professionally laid-out napkins, silver service, and glasses for water or wine, we faced the front. Next to us, a kind young couple from Arizona, understanding I was retired, asked what I would do now. I shared about having time to write, and the wife perked up. A dancer, she appreciated art and literature of any kind. We engaged in an interesting conversation.

While we talked, I noticed the mantóns de Manila or mantoncillos—Spanish flamenco shawls—draped over the backs of eight chairs in a row on the stage. *Oh my gosh,* I thought, *could it be?* Before our food arrived, I posed a question.

"What does that look like to you?" I asked the young couple next to us.

"Hmmm," the husband responded, smiling. "We'll see!"

Course after course of Spanish delights arrived, and my attention to the stage was diverted. First, the appetizer—shrimp with creamy avocado—the texture contrasting wonderfully with the shrimp, touched with lime and cilantro. The main course was delicious, tender beef with garlic mashed potatoes. The meat was juicy, perfectly cooked, and flavorful; the potatoes were creamy and topped with a delicious, rich gravy, surrounded by seasoned vegetables. Then came the most creative dessert I'd ever seen—a ball of ice cream coated with white chocolate and covered with pieces of green pistachio that made it look like a bird egg. Looking like a nest, pieces of sweet bread, red berries, tiny edible leaves, and small chocolate bits surrounded the egg. The dessert resembled something out of a fairy forest and sent up a caramelly fragrance to my nose. The combined flavor was both sweet and sour and created an indescribable taste sensation. With each bite, my mouth watered for more of the savory sweetness. At the same time, I felt my anticipation growing, and my food reverie being interrupted.

Our main course at the banquet

Suddenly, a group of people dressed in traditional Spanish attire stepped onto the stage and took their seats across the platform. After a brief introduction, the music ramped up, starting with tuning-plucks on two guitars. My heart sped up, my fingers tingled, and my ears hummed with the sound of a growing synchronized rhythm—the cadence of the Spanish guitarists. Their voices started to rise and fall as they strummed songs that reminded me of *The Gypsy Kings*—a blend of rumba, flamenco, and salsa. My heart skipped a beat, and I shuddered and shook all over. It had begun! I jumped from my seat, leaving my delicious dessert to wait, and stood by the side of the stage. I was surprised when the first dancer—a mustached man—leapt from his seat onstage. I had never witnessed a male flamenco dancer before. Dressed in a black jacket and pants, with a colorful, green-patterned shirt and tie, he swung his arms up in the air dramatically. In an adept and alluring way, he stomped his feet vigorously. Along with the guitarists, a fiery flutist highlighted the emotion of the moment, and another man passionately pounded on a flamenco cajon. Soon, a woman, who'd clapped along from her seat onstage, replaced the first dancer. She wore an embroidered navy mantoncillo to match her long, flowing, highly-decorated, multi-colored, low-cut dress. Swinging her arms, she kicked up her black-heeled shoes and stamped her feet.

Next up, a tall woman with long black hair tied back and topped with a red hair-piece stepped forward from her seat on the stage. Bearing a beautiful, royal-blue dress with black polka-dots, and swinging a lavender mantoncillo, she made the fringes furl around her as she embraced herself. Tapping her chest proudly, she hit her sides with both hands, swung her arms, and clapped her hands. It was hard not to feel what she was expressing through her movements. The rhythmic music intensified, and my heart pounded wildly with each new movement. I had a hard time keeping my feet from tapping along with the music. Standing as close as possible, I thrilled to experience the emotion of it all!

Words can't express the awe I felt. As each new dancer lunged from an onstage seat, I was completely enthralled. Sometimes with shawls, sometimes with canes twirling, sometimes mantoncillo-draped, sometimes bare-shouldered, now with a tie, now without one, each new performer held me captive. I could watch them for hours. Sadly, the show had to end. Back at my table, I took the last bites of ice cream as I watched the performers jump from the stage and walk toward me. I stood and clapped for each one as they passed by. They smiled and acknowledged my obviously overjoyed pleasure and shouted praise. *How could they know what they gave me?* I thought. I will never, ever forget this grand finale to a wonderful week in southern Spain.

Not wanting to linger because of such an early departure, we gradually got up from our seats, sipped a last taste of ruby-red Rioja, and slowly stepped through the courtyard below our balcony. I looked up and said adios to Mama Seagull, sitting far above us, surrounded by sunset colors, and I wondered if she had sent one of her hatched babies down to wish us well and let us know that someone had heard our requests. *Did she know how much I'd wanted to experience flamenco before we left?* I wondered. *Hmmm. God certainly did work in mysterious ways. I would never put it past Him to arrange this glorious night.*

As we ascended the tiled steps to our room for the last time, I wondered what magical things God had planned for us next. *Nothing would surprise me!* I smiled knowingly.

# THE END

# AFTERWORD

Two months after we returned home, I reached out to our newfound friends from the Paris airport, Lori and Mike.

"Hi, Lori," I texted. "I'm writing a book about our trip to Costa del Sol, and I included how we met you and what a God-wink that was. I mentioned how we prayed about your dream to start a couple's group, and I wondered how that's going. Let me know! I look forward to hearing your progress! Blessings! Continued prayers for you both!"

Her response was, "Mike and I are still very hopeful and passionate about a marriage mentoring ministry. We have chosen a group of people to walk alongside us as we pray for God's wisdom for what this ministry will look like. Thank you for your prayers! Let me know how I can pray for you. God bless you!"

*Please pray along with us for this evolving and much-needed marriage ministry by Lori and Mike!*

# COSTA DEL SOL-INSPIRED RECIPES THAT WILL DELIGHT YOU!

(Added recommendatons from my friend, "Chef Kay")

## CLASSIC SPANISH OMELETTE (TORTILLA ESPAÑOLA)

This is Spain's most iconic home dish—simple ingredients, perfect technique. Served warm or at room temperature, it's ideal as a tapa, light meal, or picnic dish.

### Ingredients (Serves 4–6)

- 1½ lb (700 g) **Yukon Gold or waxy potatoes**, peeled
- 1 **medium onion**, thinly sliced (optional but traditional)
- 6–8 **large eggs** (use more for a custardy center)
- 1½ cups **olive oil** (for cooking potatoes; much will be reused)
- 1½ tsp **salt**, or to taste

### Instructions

1. *Cook the Potatoes*
   - Slice potatoes thinly (⅛ inch).
   - Heat olive oil in a wide skillet over **medium-low heat**.
   - Add potatoes and onion with a pinch of salt.
   - Cook gently 15–20 minutes, **stirring often**, until soft but not browned.
   - Drain potatoes, reserving the oil.

2. *Prepare the Eggs*
   - Beat eggs in a large bowl with remaining salt.
   - Add warm potatoes and onions.

- Gently mix and let rest **5–10 minutes** (this improves texture).

3. *Cook the Tortilla*
   - Heat 2 tbsp reserved oil in a nonstick skillet (8–10 inches).
   - Pour in egg-potato mixture.
   - Cook on **medium-low** for 4–6 minutes, shaking pan occasionally, until edges set but center is soft.

4. *Flip Like a Spaniard*
   - Place a plate over the pan and flip confidently.
   - Slide tortilla back into the pan.
   - Cook 2–4 more minutes depending on desired doneness.

## Doneness Guide

- **Jugosa (slightly runny):** soft center, very traditional
- **Creamy:** fully set but custardy
- **Well-done:** firm throughout (less common in Spain)

## Variations and Suggestions

- **Tortilla de Patatas only:** skip the onion (hotly debated!)
- **With chorizo:** add sautéed chorizo slices
- **With spinach or peppers:** lightly sauté first
- **Mini tortillas:** perfect for tapas
- Serve with **aioli**, crusty bread, and marinated olives
- Pair with **Cava**, **Albariño**, or a light **Rioja**
- **Chef Kay says:** "I absolutely love this. I cooked the potatoes and onions in 3 batches and used 2 T. of olive oil and lots of salt to cook them. I sliced my potatoes on a mandaline and only cooked each batch about 10 min. This is the time consuming part. I also salted the eggs quite a bit."

# Authentic Andalusian Gazpacho (Gazpacho Andaluz)

This is the **classic summer soup of southern Spain**—cold, silky, and refreshing. True Andalusian gazpacho is simple, tomato-forward, and never chunky.

## Ingredients (Serves 4–6)

- 2 lb (900 g) **very ripe tomatoes** (Roma or vine-ripened)
- 1 **small green bell pepper**
- 1 **small garlic clove**
- ½ **medium cucumber**, peeled
- 2–3 oz (60–80 g) **day-old white bread**, crust removed
- ⅓ cup **extra-virgin olive oil** (Andalusian if possible)
- 2 tbsp **sherry vinegar** (vinagre de Jerez)
- 1 tsp **fine sea salt**, to taste
- Cold water, only if needed (traditional versions use none)

## Preparation

1. *Prepare the Bread*
   - Soak bread briefly in water.
   - Squeeze out excess completely.

2. *Blend*
   - Add tomatoes, pepper, cucumber, garlic, bread, vinegar, and salt to a blender.
   - Blend until completely smooth (1–2 minutes).

3. *Emulsify*
   - With the blender running, **slowly drizzle in olive oil**.
   - This creates the signature creamy texture.

4. *Strain (Traditional but Optional)*
   - Pass through a fine sieve for **ultra-smooth gazpacho**, especially common in Andalucía.

5. *Chill*
   - Refrigerate at least **2 hours**.
   - Adjust salt and vinegar just before serving.

## How It's Served in Andalusía

- **In a glass**, like a drink
- Or in a bowl with classic *tropezones*:
  - Finely diced cucumber
  - Green pepper
  - Croutons
  - Hard-boiled egg (optional)

## Andalusian Tips

- Tomatoes should be **sweet, not acidic**
- Garlic should be barely noticeable
- Olive oil quality matters more than anything
- Never add onions in traditional versions
- Ice cubes dilute flavor—always chill instead
- Pairs beautifully with **Manzanilla sherry** or **dry fino**
- **Chef Kay says:** "I don't think it needs the bread, it's thick enough. I only added 1 T. olive oil."

# Andalusian Grilled Turbot (Rodaballo a la Brasa)

## Philosophy (very important in Andalusia)

No heavy marinades. No sauces masking the fish. Just **fire, salt, olive oil, and restraint**—with a light garlic finish added at the end.

**Serves: 2–4**

## Ingredients

### For the fish

- 1 whole turbot (rodaballo), **2–3 lb / 1–1.5 kg**, cleaned
- Coarse sea salt (preferably *sal gruesa*)
- Extra-virgin olive oil
- 1 lemon, halved

### Classic Andalusian garlic finish

- 5 tbsp extra-virgin olive oil
- 3–4 garlic cloves, thinly sliced
- 1 tbsp finely chopped flat-leaf parsley
- Optional: pinch of **sweet smoked paprika (pimentón dulce)**

### To serve

- Boiled or roasted new potatoes
- Grilled lemon halves
- Simple tomato salad with olive oil and flaky salt

## Method

1. *Prepare the turbot*
   - Pat the fish very dry.
   - Score the **dark (top) skin** with 2–3 shallow diagonal cuts.
   - Rub lightly with olive oil and generously season with coarse sea salt on both sides.
   - Let rest at room temperature for **15 minutes** before grilling.

2. *Heat the grill (authentic way)*
   - **Charcoal grill preferred**, medium-high heat.
   - The embers should be glowing, not flaming.
   - Oil the grates well—Andalusian grilling relies on clean release.

3. *Grill the fish*
   - Place turbot **dark skin side down** first.
   - Grill **8–10 minutes without moving** until the skin is crisp and releases naturally.
   - Carefully flip (two wide spatulas help).
   - Grill another **6–8 minutes** until just cooked through.

   **Doneness cue:**
   - The flesh should be pearly, juicy, and gently pulling from the bone (about **130–135°F / 54–57°C** at the thickest point).
   - Rest the fish **3–5 minutes** off the grill.

4. *Make the garlic oil (ajillo)*
   - Warm olive oil gently over low heat.
   - Add garlic slices and cook **just until pale gold**—never brown.
   - Remove from heat; stir in parsley and optional paprika.
   - Spoon lightly over the fish right before serving.
   - Finish with fresh lemon juice at the table.

## How it's served in Málaga

- Presented **whole**, then filleted tableside.
- Garlic oil added sparingly—never drowning the fish.
- Potatoes served plain to soak up olive oil and juices.

## Wine pairing (Andalusian authentic choices)

- **Dry Málaga white** (Moscatel de Alejandría)
- **Albariño** (Rías Baixas)
- **Verdejo** (Rueda)
- **Fino or Manzanilla Sherry** (well chilled)

# Mediterranean Sautéed Eggplant (Gaia Restaurant-Inspired)

## Ingredients (serves 4 as an appetizer)

- 2 medium eggplants (~800 g), cut into ½-inch (1–1.5 cm) cubes or slices
- 4–5 Tbsp extra-virgin olive oil
- 3 garlic cloves, thinly sliced
- 1 small shallot or ½ small red onion, finely chopped
- 1 Tbsp white miso paste (optional, for depth of flavor)
- ¼ cup dry white wine or vegetable stock
- Zest and juice of ½ lemon
- 1–2 Tbsp red wine vinegar or sherry vinegar
- 1–2 tsp honey or a pinch of sugar (optional)
- 2 Tbsp fresh parsley, chopped
- 1 Tbsp fresh mint or dill, chopped (optional)
- Sea salt and black pepper to taste
- Optional garnishes: toasted pine nuts, crumbled feta cheese, pomegranate seeds

## Instructions

1. *Prepare the eggplant:*
   - Sprinkle cubed/ sliced eggplant with a little salt and let sit in a colander for 20–30 min to draw out bitterness. Rinse and pat dry with paper towels.

2. *Sauté aromatics:*
   - In a large skillet over medium heat, warm 3–4 Tbsp of olive oil. Add the garlic and shallot and gently cook until fragrant and translucent (about 1–2 minutes).

3.  *Cook the eggplant:*
    - Add the eggplant to the skillet and stir to coat with the oil and aromatics.
    - Season with salt and pepper. Cook for about 8–10 min until the eggplant begins to soften and caramelize. If the pan looks dry, add a splash more oil.

4.  *Deglaze & flavor:*
    - Stir in the white wine or stock to deglaze the pan, scraping up any browned bits.
    - Mix in the miso paste (if using) until dissolved and well combined.

5.  *Brighten the dish:*
    - Add the vinegar, lemon zest, lemon juice, and honey (if using). Cook another 2–3 min to let flavors meld and liquid reduce slightly.

6.  *Finish & serve:*
    - Remove from heat. Stir in fresh parsley (and mint/dill if using).
    - Transfer to a serving plate. Garnish with toasted pine nuts, crumbled feta, or pomegranate seeds for a festive touch.

## Serving Suggestions

- Serve warm or at room temperature with:
    - Crusty bread or grilled pita
    - Greek yogurt or whipped feta dip
    - Olives and fresh tomatoes
    - As part of a meze platter
    - **Chef Kay says:** "I made this exactly like written. I kept adding more honey and lemon juice to bring the flavor up, but there is something still missing in my opinion. I added a drizzle of balsamic vinegar the next night and it was better."

# Wine pairing

- **Albariño** (Rías Baixas)
- **Verdejo** (Rueda)
- **Assyrtiko** (Greece)
- **Dry Moscatel** (Málaga, Andalusia)
- **Garnacha** (Grenache)
- **Frappato** (Sicily)
- **Cinsault**
- **Dry Sherry** – Fino or Manzanilla

# Mediterranean Truffle Pasta (Elegant & Simple)

This Mediterranean-style truffle pasta highlights **quality olive oil, butter, cheese, and fresh herbs**, letting the truffle aroma shine without heaviness.

**Serves:** 2–3. **Time:** 20 minutes

## Ingredients

- 8 oz (225 g) fresh pasta (tagliolini, fettuccine, or linguine)
- 2 Tbsp extra-virgin olive oil
- 1 Tbsp unsalted butter
- 1 small garlic clove, lightly crushed (optional, subtle)
- 2–3 Tbsp truffle oil **or** ½–1 fresh black truffle, finely shaved
- ¼ cup finely grated Parmigiano Reggiano or Pecorino Romano
- 2–3 Tbsp pasta cooking water (as needed)
- Sea salt and freshly ground black pepper
- Optional finishing herbs: fresh parsley or thyme (very sparingly)
- Optional garnish: lemon zest (a whisper)

## Instructions

1. *Cook the pasta*
   - Bring well-salted water to a boil. Cook pasta until just al dente. Reserve ½ cup of the cooking water before draining.

2. *Build the base*
   - In a wide pan over low heat, warm the olive oil and butter. Add the crushed garlic and gently infuse for 30–45 seconds; remove garlic (keep it delicate).

3. *Emulsify*
   - Add 2 Tbsp pasta water to the pan and swirl to create a light emulsion.

4. *Combine*
   - Add drained pasta to the pan. Toss gently over low heat, adding more pasta water if needed to keep it silky.

5. *Truffle moment*
   - Remove from heat. Stir in truffle oil **or** add shaved fresh truffle. Season lightly with salt and pepper.

6. *Finish*
   - Fold in grated cheese until glossy and coated. Taste and adjust seasoning.

## To Serve

- Plate immediately.
- Top with extra truffle shavings or a few drops of truffle oil.
- Add a *tiny* pinch of herbs or lemon zest if desired.

## Chef's Tips

- **Less is more:** Truffle flavor should whisper, not shout.
- **Heat control:** Always add truffle off heat to preserve aroma.
- **Mediterranean balance:** Olive oil leads; butter supports.

## Variations

- **Truffle & Mushroom:** Sauté thinly sliced wild mushrooms in olive oil first.
- **Truffle Lemon:** Add a teaspoon of lemon juice at the end for brightness.
- **Vegan:** Skip butter and cheese; use great olive oil, nutritional yeast, and fresh truffle.
- **Chef Kay says,** "Add truffle salt to taste to add even more flavor."

## Wine Pairing

- **Godello** (Valdeorras or Bierzo)
- **White Rioja** (Viura-based, lightly oaked)
- **Albariño** (Rías Baixas)
- **Xarel·lo** (Penedès, still—not Cava)
- **Garnacha Blanca** (Terra Alta)
- **Mencía** (Bierzo)
- **Garnacha** (Old-vine, low oak)
- **Trepat** (Catalonia)
- **Cava Reserva / Gran Reserva** (Brut Nature)
- **Sherry** – Amontillado

# Andalusian Black Paella (Arroz Negro Andaluz)

A coastal specialty from southern Spain, rich with squid ink, seafood, and deep Mediterranean flavor.

## Ingredients (serves 4)

### For the base
- 2 cups **bomba rice** (or calasparra rice)
- 4½–5 cups **fish stock**, hot
- 2 sachets **squid ink** (about 8–10 g total)
- 4 tbsp **extra-virgin olive oil**

### Seafood
- 12–16 **fresh prawns**, shell on
- 10 oz (300 g) **squid**, cleaned and sliced into rings
- Optional (very Andalusian): a handful of **clams or mussels**

### Sofrito
- 1 medium **onion**, finely chopped
- 4 cloves **garlic**, minced
- 1 small **green bell pepper**, finely diced
- 1 medium **ripe tomato**, grated
- 1 tsp **sweet smoked paprika** (pimentón dulce)
- ½ tsp **ñora pepper paste** or a pinch of dried ñora flesh (optional but traditional)
- Salt to taste

### To finish
- Fresh **parsley**, finely chopped
- **Lemon wedges**
- Optional but classic: **allioli** (garlic mayonnaise)

## Method

*1.   Prepare the ink stock*

Dissolve the squid ink into the hot fish stock, whisking well. Keep warm over low heat.

*2.   Sauté the seafood*

Heat olive oil in a wide paella pan over medium-high heat.
  * Quickly sear the prawns until just pink. Remove and set aside.
  * Add the squid, sauté 1–2 minutes until opaque. Remove and set aside.

*3.   Make the sofrito*

Lower heat to medium. In the same pan:
  * Add onion and bell pepper; cook slowly until soft and lightly golden (8–10 minutes).
  * Add garlic; cook 30 seconds.
  * Stir in grated tomato and ñora. Cook until thick and jammy.
  * Add smoked paprika, stirring quickly so it doesn't burn.

*4.   Add rice & ink stock*
  * Stir in the rice, coating every grain with the sofrito (1–2 minutes).
  * Pour in the hot squid-ink stock evenly.
  * Season lightly with salt (the ink adds salinity).

**Do not stir again.**
  * Bring to a gentle boil, then reduce to medium-low and cook **15–18 minutes.**

*5.   Finish the paella*
  * At minute 10, nestle the squid and clams/mussels into the rice.
  * In the final 3–4 minutes, place the prawns on top.
  * Increase heat briefly at the end to form a **light socarrat** (crispy bottom).

*6. Rest & serve*

Remove from heat, cover loosely with a cloth, and rest **5 minutes**. Finish with parsley and lemon wedges. Serve with **allioli on the side**, as is common along the Andalusian coast.

## Andalusian Tips

- Black paella in Andalusia is **lighter and more seafood-forward** than some Catalan versions.
- Olive oil is generous but never greasy.
- The rice should be **dry and separate**, never creamy.

## Wine Pairing

- **Most traditional:** Manzanilla
- **Elegant & classic:** Fino Sherry
- **Fresh & modern:** Albariño
- **Budget-friendly:** Verdejo or Muscadet

# Greek-Mediterranean Roasted Chicken (Gaia Restaurant-Inspired)

**Serves:** 4. **Time:** 1 hour

## Ingredients

- 1 whole chicken (about 3–4 lb / 1.4–1.8 kg), spatchcocked or quartered
- 3–4 Tbsp extra-virgin olive oil
- 4 garlic cloves, thinly sliced
- 1 lemon (zest + juice)
- 1 orange (optional, zest + juice for extra citrus brightness)
- 2 tsp dried oregano (or 1 Tbsp fresh)
- 1–2 tsp fresh thyme leaves (or rosemary)
- 1 tsp smoked paprika (optional)
- Sea salt and freshly ground black pepper
- 1 cup cherry tomatoes
- ½ cup Kalamata olives (pitted)
- ½ cup white wine or chicken stock
- Fresh parsley and/or fresh oregano to garnish

## Instructions

1. *Prep the Chicken*
   - **Preheat oven:** 425°F (220°C).
   - **Prepare chicken:** Pat the chicken dry with paper towels. If spatchcocking, remove backbone and flatten; if quartering, just make sure pieces are even.
   - **Season:** Rub the chicken all over with olive oil. Sprinkle generously with salt, pepper, oregano, thyme, and smoked paprika (if using). Scatter lemon zest over the chicken.

2. *Flavor Base*
   - **Aromatics:** Place garlic slices under the skin and over the top of the chicken.
   - **Citrus:** Squeeze lemon (and orange, if using) juice over the chicken and into the cavity/around the pieces.

3. *Roast*
   - **Arrange:** Place the chicken skin-side up in a roasting pan or cast-iron skillet.
   - **Add vegetables & fruit:** Nestle cherry tomatoes and Kalamata olives around the chicken.
   - **Deglaze:** Pour white wine or chicken stock into the pan (this keeps the chicken moist and creates a fragrant pan sauce).
   - **Roast:** Bake for about **45–55 minutes**, or until the internal temperature reaches 165°F (74°C) and the skin is golden and crispy. Baste once halfway through with the pan juices.

4. *Rest & Serve*
   - **Rest:** Let the chicken rest 10 minutes before carving.
   - **Garnish:** Sprinkle with fresh parsley (and extra lemon slices if you like).
   - **Chef Kay says:** "This is the moistest chicken I've ever had ( I don't buy chicken with the skin on). Very good, only thing I would do is put alot of salt and herbs under the skin. I did spatchcock the chicken and made it exactly like written."
   - **Serve with:**
     - **Roasted or grilled vegetables** (zucchini, eggplant, peppers)
     - **Greek salad** with tomatoes, cucumber, red onion, and feta
     - **Warm pita or crusty bread** to soak up the juices

## Wine Pairing

- **Dry Spanish white** (Albariño or Verdejo)
- **Greek Assyrtiko** for crisp minerality
- **Rosé** for a versatile, refreshing complement

# COCONUT SORBET WITH PINEAPPLE, TOASTED ALMOND, CHOCOLATE & MINT

A light, elegant dessert—refreshing, aromatic, and perfectly balanced.

## COCONUT SORBET

### Ingredients (Serves 6)

- 2 cups **full-fat coconut milk**
- ¾ cup **coconut water**
- ½ cup **sugar** (or ⅓ cup honey or agave)
- Pinch of **fine sea salt**
- Zest of **½ lime**
- 1 tbsp **fresh lime juice**

### Method

1. *Heat coconut milk, coconut water, sugar, and salt just until sugar dissolves.*

2. *Remove from heat; stir in lime zest and juice.*

3. *Chill completely (at least 4 hours).*

4. *Churn in an ice-cream maker until smooth and scoopable.*
   - *No machine?* Freeze flat, stirring every 30–40 minutes until smooth

## TOPPINGS & GARNISH

- 1 cup **fresh pineapple**, cut into very small cubes
- ¼ cup **raw almonds**, finely chopped
- 2 oz **dark chocolate (70%)**, finely chopped or shaved
- 2 tbsp **fresh mint**, finely chopped
- **Lime wedges**, for serving

## Prepare the Toppings

- Toast almonds in a dry pan over medium heat until golden and fragrant. Cool.
- Keep pineapple chilled and well-drained for clean presentation.

## To Assemble

- Scoop coconut sorbet into chilled bowls or plates.
- Sprinkle with pineapple cubes.
- Add toasted almond and dark chocolate bits.
- Finish with chopped mint.
- Serve with a **lime wedge** on the side—guests squeeze just before eating.

## Chef's Notes

- Cut pineapple **very small**—this keeps the dessert refined and balanced.
- Use **high-quality dark chocolate** for a subtle bitterness.
- Mint should be fresh and restrained—aroma, not dominance.
- Chill serving plates for a restaurant-style finish.
- **Chef Kay says:** "This was delicious and easy. I did not add mint. I have a small Cuisinart ice cream maker I made it in. I added toppings of pineapple, almonds and chocolate, but next time I would stir some coconut and almonds into the batter."

## Optional Pairings

- Sparkling water with lime
- Moscato d'Asti or late-harvest Riesling
- Coconut water with fresh mint

# Acknowledgements

My heartfelt thanks go to a few people, whose willingness to read my manuscript and give me needed feedback is so very much appreciated. Their comments and input enabled me to finetune the document, especially the details, thus making each excursion and scenario come alive in a greater way. Thank you to Bret Kolman, Andrea Jeselnik, Julia Ogutu, and Brian Skillen. Your kind words and helpful suggestions have meant so much to me! Many thanks to "Chef" Kay Klement for her invaluable input on the Andalusian recipes. Her suggestions will be very helpful for those who want to try them out. I also want to acknowledge Brian Skillen and his staff at Publishing Hackers for their incredible assistance and remarkable patience and diligence in helping to make this book come to life! And many thanks to Lori and Mike, who allowed me to include some of their story in this book. I appreciate all who have touched this story! God bless you!

# ABOUT THE AUTHOR

**Lele Beutel** and her husband, Mike, enjoy traveling to new places. They have found that, with each excursion, come opportunities to make a difference in people's lives and have their own lives changed as a result. Walking on the Cotswolds was one such adventure for Lele. She considers herself to be a "secret agent" for God because of how He often leads her into unexpected situations where she's able to connect with others. Before retirement, she spent 25 years as a financial advisor and was able to encourage many people mentally, spiritually, and financially through her faith-based advice. Now, she and her husband spend time with their two dogs, Andey and Barney, with grandkids, and as volunteers at their church. They also share experiences with their church life-group members and the neighbors they meet while walking the dogs.

Other books she has written include: *Lessons from the Cotswolds, Two Old Fogies Dodge Disasters while Walking through the Cotswolds; The Camino Connection, Connecting with Life and Commemorating a Death While Walking on the Camino de Santiago; What God Wants You to Know, A Daily Devotional; God Answers, A Daily Devotional for Christians; Lele's Selah: Prayerful Poems that Inspire Hope,* and *Flora's Story, A young girl and her family survive the Nazi and Russian regimes of 1940s Germany.*

To reach her, you can find her on Facebook.
Or email her at: apedersen6@comcast.net.
She would love to hear from you!